Understanding
GABRIEL GARCÍA MÁRQUEZ

UNDERSTANDING CONTEMPORARY EUROPEAN and LATIN AMERICAN LITERATURE

JAMES HARDIN, *SERIES EDITOR*

* * * * *

Understanding Günter Grass
by Alan Frank Keele

Understanding Graciliano Ramos
by Celso Lemos de Oliveira

Understanding Gabriel García Márquez
by Kathleen McNerney

UNDERSTANDING

GABRIEL GARCÍA MÁRQUEZ

KATHLEEN MCNERNEY

UNIVERSITY OF SOUTH CAROLINA PRESS

Copyright © University of South Carolina 1989

Published in Columbia, South Carolina, by the
University of South Carolina Press

Manufactured in the United States of America

Second Printing, 1990

LIBRARY OF CONGRESS
Library of Congress Cataloging-in-Publication Data

McNerney, Kathleen.
 Understanding Gabriel García Márquez.

 (Understanding contemporary European and Latin
American literature)
  Bibliography: p.
  Includes index.
  1. García Márquez, Gabriel, 1928–   —Criticism
and interpretation. I. Title. II. Series.
PQ8180.17.A73Z724 1989   863   88-27829
ISBN 0-87249-563-9
ISBN 0-87249-564-7 (pbk.)

To all those who work toward social justice in Latin America, and to those who will benefit by their success

CONTENTS

CONTENTS

EDITOR'S PREFACE

UNDERSTANDING CONTEMPORARY EUROPEAN AND LATIN American Literature has been planned as a series of guides for students and nonacademic readers. Like its companion series, *Understanding Contemporary American Literature*, the aim of the books is to provide a brief introduction to the life and writings of prominent contemporary authors and to explicate their most important works.

Contemporary literature makes special demands, and this is particularly true of foreign literature, in which the reader must contend only with unfamiliar, often arcane artistic conventions and philosophical concepts, but also with the handicap of reading the literature in translation. It is a truism that the nuances of the language can be rendered in another only imperfectly (and this problem is especially difficult in fiction), but the fact that the words of European and Latin American writers are situated in a historical and cultural setting quite different from our own can be as great a hindrance to the understanding of these works as the linguistic barrier. For this reason, the *UCELL* series will emphasize the sociological and historical background of the writers treated. The peculiar philosophical and cultural traditions of a given culture may be particularly important for an understanding of certain authors, and these will be taken up in the introductory chapter and also in the discussion of these works in which this information is relevant. Beyond this, the books will treat the specifically literary aspects of the author under discussion and attempt to explain the complexities of contemporary literature lucidly. The books are conceived as introductions to the authors covered, not as comprehensive analyses. They do not provide summaries of plot, as they are meant to be used in conjunction with the books they treat, not as a substitute for the study of the original works.

It is our hope that the *UCELL* series will help to increase our understanding of the European and Latin American cultures and will serve to make the path to the literature of those cultures more accessible.

J.H.

PREFACE AND
ACKNOWLEDGMENTS

EVEN IF GABRIEL GARCÍA MÁRQUEZ HAD NOT WON THE Nobel Prize in 1982, he would still be of the greatest interest to readers in the United States. As one of the world's best known and loved living authors, his novel *One Hundred Years of Solitude* had sold 30 million copies in 36 languages by its twentieth anniversary in 1987.

The term *magic realism* is not as popular today as it once was, but it still aptly describes much of García Márquez's fiction and prepares the reader a bit for what to expect. Although the writer himself says that he doesn't exaggerate or make things up, a reader accustomed to the realism of earlier fiction will do well to begin García Márquez with a willing suspension of disbelief. Things happen on a colossal scale, and Macondo, where much of his fiction takes place, is no ordinary small town. García Márquez is a master at telling us universal truths that amaze us with candor and charm. His matter-of-fact style of narrating the most incredible happenings makes everything seem possible, and indeed inevitable.

To be read for its literary value, of course, the work of García Márquez, especially his novels, also gives us a kind of history lesson of Latin America. This is a particularly valuable lesson today, for he describes the social reality and background of his country, and by analogy other similar countries, with vigor and truth.

The deserved popularity of Gabriel García Márquez made the experience of working on this book especially gratifying, for many friends and colleagues knew his work and offered enthusiastic support and helpful suggestions. I would like to thank Enrique Pupo-Walker, Patsy Boyer, and Pablo González for their insightful remarks on the man, his country, and his literature; Sharon Goodman, Cristina Enríquez de Salamanca, and Carles Pedrós-Alió for many useful conversations; Luis and Julio González for their help with the bibliography; Barbara Reider for her patient typing and corrections; and especially John Martin, for a little of all of the above plus constant help and encouragement.

Understanding
GABRIEL GARCÍA MÁRQUEZ

The Man and His Country

Speaking of Latin America often results in an abundant use of superlatives: the widest river, the longest chain of tall mountains, the driest desert, the rainiest forest, the greatest waterfalls. Contrasts, too, come easily: fabulous wealth and abject poverty, refined culture and illiteracy, gay folk dances and bloody massacres, bright flowered shirts and the black garb of widows, traditional parliamentary systems and unspeakably cruel dictatorships.

Colombia reflects both superlatives and contrasts in many ways. By no means the largest country of the continent, it nonetheless covers 1,138,914 square kilometers—more than Texas, Oklahoma, Arkansas, and Louisiana taken together. The major river system, the Magdalena, finds most of the population along or near its banks; its Andean peaks contrast not only with river valleys and plains but even more so with the tropical coastal area more akin to its neighbors in the Caribbean. Colombian history reads like a series of adventure tales, imaginative and somewhat exaggerated. Indian tribes of several different groups, Spanish conquistadors, pirates and smugglers, slave traders and idealistic fighters for independence from Spain, regional strongmen, mercenaries for battles and big-time tyrants, fine lyric poets and greedy capitalists and cocaine kings—all weave together

3

a pattern of history unique in some ways but all too representative of the South American continent as a whole.

The major pre-Columbian inhabitants were mainly Caribs along the coasts and Chibchas and Quechuas in the interior. Although this last group was related to the Inca, the area was too far north to form part of the great empire whose center was Cuzco in Peru. The Caribs were reputed to be fierce and aggressive. The only descendants of these early peoples are the Guajiro, a very small percentage of the population, who still inhabit the coastal plains of their ancestors.

The first Spaniards came in 1500; Santa Marta was founded in 1525, Cartagena in 1533, and Bogotá in 1538. An easy conquest led to the formation of the Nuevo Reino de Granada, with its governing body in Bogotá. Despite its administrative and judicial powers over the whole of Nueva Granada, it ultimately depended on the viceroy of Peru.

The sixteenth and seventeenth centuries were chaotic as a result of the destruction of the indigenous systems of commerce, which led to a fragmented society and local rule in some areas. Nueva Granada was received by the formation of the new Bourbon viceroyalty in 1717, and colonial sectors profited and prospered greatly, basing their economy on agriculture, mining, textiles, and commerce, depending on the area. The cultural level was elevated as well, with the backing of a number of learned viceroys; teaching flourished, and cultural institutions were born among colonial inhabitants that survive today.

Nevertheless, symptoms of rebellion can be detected as early as 1780, and the French Revolution provided further impetus for open revolt. Although 1810 is the official date of independence, the fighting was just beginning. A proclamation of independence of the Provincias Unidas de Nueva Granada was issued in 1813, but fights raged between independentists and royalists, between centralists and federalists, and between the colonial forces of Spain and the freedom fighters. The Venezuelan Simón Bolívar, with help from the British, entered the capital in 1819, ending the fighting; the Republic of Gran Colombia was declared, including the territories of Venezuela, Ecuador, and Peru was well as Colombia. It took another three years to secure these adjacent regions; in the meantime tensions between centralists and regionalists resulted in the separation of the other three countries from Gran Colombia, leaving what is now Colombia.

A continuous series of civil wars finally culminated in the devastating War of One Thousand Days, which ended in 1903 after claiming more than 100,000 lives and contributing to Columbia's loss of Panama. The period of relative calm that followed was still characterized by the historic rivalry between the liberals, with strongholds in the capital and the coastal zones, and the conservatives, with strength along the river valleys and the southern mountains. The two sides traded power more or less peacefully until a populist threatened to make some real changes in the system; in 1948 Jorge Eliécer Gaitán was assassinated, and the decade that followed was so bloody it was called, simply, The Violence, claiming an estimated 300,000 lives.[1] The dictatorship that resulted gave way to another uneasy pact between liberals and conservatives.

5

The problems common to the South American continent characterize Colombia today: the huge gap between the rich and the poor and the social injustice that goes with it; economic control by multinational companies; dependence on coffee with its fluctuating prices; the tremendous power of the cocaine mafia; a still underdeveloped system of communication and transportation; and the presence of guerrilla forces. Despite these colossal problems the constitutional system struggles along.

The duality that forms Colomia is reflected in its people; many Colombians would agree that they come in two basic varieties: the highlanders and those from the coast. The differences in types of popular music are symbolic illustrations: while the gay, carefree, rhythmic cumbia, with its African influences, and the national dance that goes with it, characterize the Caribbean coast, slow-moving, almost funereal music is more typical of the highlands. The courtesy and formalism of the mountains may conceal repressed aggressions; political violence in the country usually has its source in this area.

Bogotá is a chilly mountain city with plenty of rain; Barranquilla is a tropical Caribbean port. The northernmost province of the country—and indeed of the continent—called La Guajira after its primitive inhabitants, is rich in history, legend, and lore. One of the least populated areas of the country, it was visited by Sir Francis Drake and other fortune seekers.

Gabriel García Márquez was born in the small town of Aracataca, in the province of La Guajira, in 1928.[2] His father, a telegraphist and an outsider to the area, did not meet with the immediate approval of his wife's family, an important one in the village. The couple moved to another town, but Gabriel's mother returned for the birth of her first child, Gabriel himself. She then went back to her husband, leaving the baby with his grandparents. He stayed there until the death of his grandfather when he was eight years old; we hope García Márquez is exaggerating when he says nothing interesting has happened to him since that time.[3]

And indeed it must have been a tremendous childhood. His grandfather, Colonel Nicolás Márquez Iguarán, had participated in the civil wars at the turn of the century and had many a tale to tell. His grandmother, Tranquilina Iguarán Cotes, populated the rambling house with otherworldly beings which fascinated as well as frightened the youngster. If many of the tales he heard during this period find their way into his fiction, it is the matter-of-fact tone with which his grandmother said the most outrageous things that characterizes his work. As García Márquez has pointed out, both grandparents were descendants of Galicians, great yarn spinners remotely related to the Celts.

García Márquez seldom actually lived with his large family—fifteen siblings, among them, another Gabriel. He studied briefly in Barranquilla but soon went to Zipaquira, near the capital, to finish his degree. It seemed the saddest city in the world to him; the contrast between the mountains and his native Caribbean must have been a shock. Nevertheless he continued his studies at the University of Bogotá, beginning with law and ending as a journalist. He began to contribute occasional stories to *El Espectador*, one of two major daily papers of the country. He moved in Cartagena and then Barranquilla, but returned to Bogotá in 1954, when he became a regular reporter for the paper, all the while continuing to write stories. The year 1955 marks the beginning of his literary career, for he published his first book, *La hojarasca (Leaf Storm)* and won a prize from the Association of Artists and Writers of Bogotá for his story "Isabel viendo llover en Macondo," ("Monologue of Isabel Watching It Rain in Macondo"). It was also the year of his first trip to Europe. Still working for *El Espectador*, he went to Geneva and then Paris, but the paper was closed shortly thereafter by the dictator Rojas Pinilla and he was left with his period of poverty in the French capital, common to so many artists and writers, though he firmly believes one writes better when well-fed. To make matters worse, he was often mistaken for an Algerian in this tense period of the death throes of French colonialism. He finally ended up helping the Algerian cause, not to give lie to the suspicions of the French police.

Surviving at least in part due to an understanding landlady, he worked on a manuscript that finally evolved into two short novels, *La mala hora (In Evil Hour)* and *El coronel no tiene quien le escriba (No One Writes to the Colonel)*, this latter story having superimposed itself over the first. Finished with *No One Writes to the Colonel*, he traveled through Eastern Europe the following year and wrote reports about that experience; then he returned to Latin America to work as a reporter in Caracas.

As a student and reporter in Barranquilla during what was surely one of the most stimulating periods of his life, he was part of a group of young men, all passionate about literature, who met frequently and spoke of little else. The members of that group were especially interested in William Faulkner, James Joyce, and Ernest Hemingway; he fell in love with Virginia Woolf as well. Under the tutelage of a Catalan exile who ran an impressive bookstore and wrote plays, García Márquez and his companions discovered many authors, both classic and modern. The revelation of Kafka's *Metamorphosis*, in which a man becomes an insect, led him to take writing more seriously; if, after all, Kafka could turn a person into a bug, maybe his own ideas weren't so farfetched. But above all, and again with some specific suggestions from the bookshop owner Ramón Vinyes, he read poetry.

That young journalist, who lived in poverty in a hotel-brothel, in a different room every night—or morning, since he usually worked, talked, drank, and read until morning—also met in Barranquilla a young pharmacist named Mercedes Barcha. In 1958, fourteen years after his original proposal, after his travels in Europe and with the prospect of a steady job in Caracas, he married her. During this period he sold encyclopedias and medical books and wrote most of the stories that would appear in *Los funerales de la Mamá Grande (Big Mama's Funeral)*.

Enthusiastic about the Cuban Revolution of 1959, he began to work for the news agency Prensa Latina, a job that took him to Bogotá, Havana, and New York. He and his family received threats from Cuban exiles, but his leaving this job in 1961 was a result of strife within the organization.

He moved to Mexico, but not directly. With Mercedes and their infant son, and almost no money, he took a trip by Greyhound bus through the South. He was especially anxious to see and feel Faulkner's Mississippi, and indeed discovered something important there that he believed he and the famous American writer shared: their roots in the Caribbean. The dusty roads of what could have been Yoknapatawpha Country looked extremely familiar to him, and he arrived in Mexico freshly inspired.

In addition to his love for Mercedes, his son, and poetry, Gabriel García Márquez was also addicted to film. During his years in Europe he had studied cinema briefly in Italy. Now in Mexico he began to write film scripts and continued his work as journalist and public relations agent. Then, suddenly having figured out how to put together the novel that had been in his head for years, he turned around from a vacation trip and secluded himself for eighteen months. The result, in 1967, was *Cien años de soledad (One Hundred Years of Solitude)*. The family—there were two boys by now—was so poor and so far in debt by the time he finished that they could barely scrape together the postage to send it to Argentina for publication. It was an immediate and tremendous success, no doubt to Mercedes's great relief.

Having been previously rejected by a publisher in Barcelona but enthusiastically previewed in sections by well-known Latin American writers, *One Hundred Years of Solitude* won for its author a number of prizes. It has been repeatedly reprinted. The notoriety ended García Márquez's economic problems forever, but it also interfered greatly with his private life. As a journalist himself, he used to grant many interviews and was generous with reporters in general. But when the interview–conference cycle became oppressive and showed no signs of letting up, he began to guard more and more jealously the little private time he had. For a while he alternated residence between Mexico and Barcelona with frequent trips to Colombia. In 1972 he published the short novel *La increíble y triste historia de la cándida Eréndira y de su abuela desalmada (The Incredible and Sad Tale of Innocent Erendira and Her Heartless Grandmother)* and the following year a compilation of some of his early journalistic articles with a telling title: *Cuando era feliz e indocumentado* (When I was happy and undocumented). He founded a magazine, *Alternativa*, in 1974 and worked on his second major novel, *El otoño del patriarca (The Autumn of the Patriarch)*, in the grand tradition of Latin American dictator novels, which came out in 1975. Continuing with journalism as well as fiction, he produced a study of Cuba's role in Africa in 1977 called *Operación* *Carlota (Operation Carlota)*. Splendidly blending his two genres of writing, he published a novel in 1981 that reads like a sensational newspaper article, and indeed is based on just that. *Crónica de una muerte anunciada (Chronicle of a Death Foretold)* is a story that happened in the town of Sucre when García Márquez lived there briefly as a young man. In preparation for the novel he reread old accounts and interviewed people involved in a case that has to be characterized as prototypically Latin American. In 1982 Gariel García Márquez was awarded the Nobel Prize for Literature. He attended the award ceremony in Stockholm in December, dressed as a casual Caribbean partygoer, and spoke of poetry and world peace.

If irony is one of his most enduring techniques and effective methods of battle, one can only imagine the glee that accompanied him and his friend Graham Greene to

Washington in 1978 as negotiators of the Panama Canal Treaty. Both writers have great difficulties, as absurd as they are tenacious, with entry into the United States. As friends of the last Panamanian leader Omar Torrijos, smugly disdained as a dictator by many, they were invited to the United States as diplomats and greeted with full fanfare. It is one of the few occasions on which Gabriel García Márquez has had official recognition for his role as mediator.[4]

While he lived in Spain, García Márquez began an occasional collaboration with the leading Spanish newspaper, *El País*. He still contributes articles once in a while, and has published stories there as well. In 1986 he gave a moving speech in Mexico against world armament before the Group of Six for Peace and Disarmament (Mexico, Argentina, Greece, Sweden, India, and Tanzania) which *El País* published; the paper also ran a series of articles about the secret visit to Chile of the exiled filmmaker Miguel Littín, who filmed, under an assumed identity and most difficult and dangerous conditions, six hours of edited footage inside Chile so the world could get a good look at the current dictatorship of Augusto Pinochet. *El País* later published this series in book form: *La aventura de Miguel Littín clandestino en Chile (Clandestine in Chile: The Adventures of Miguel Littín)*. The book went through three editions within a few months—helped, perhaps, by the burning of some 15,000 copies by the supporters of Pinochet in Santiago who felt threatened by such exposure.

This work is indicative of García Márquez's commitment to activist politics. A leftist since his formative years, he believes his contributions are in the following

12

areas: first, the writing of good literature, not necessarily what would be termed social literature; second, the type of journalism that exposes the horrors and injustices in Latin America and keeps them present in our collective consciousness; and third, a sort of underground diplomacy he finds himself in a unique and ideal position to practice. He has worked in favor of peace, disarmament, and human rights, he has negotiated the release of hostages held by guerrilla forces; and he has founded publications, with money from literary prizes, in an effort to offer an alternative press to the "official story" found in so many major news sources.

If fame and fortune have troubled his private life, they have also made possible some of this work to which he is so firmly committed. His list of friends—and friendship is an extremely important value for him—is impressive and varied. Among them he counts French President François Mitterand and Cuban Prime Minister Fidel Castro, with whom he discusses seafood and literature, and various writers from Latin America and elsewhere, including Carlos Fuentes and Graham Greene. He has lost some important friends. Pablo Neruda died shortly after Pinochet took over in Chile; Omar Torrijos of Panama was killed in a plane crash in 1981, which García Márquez is not convinced was an accident. Camilo Torres, who baptized his son, was an early loss; this priest-revolutionary was killed by Colombian soldiers in 1968. A recent loss is Olof Palme of Sweden, assassinated under unexplained circumstances in 1986.

García Márquez finds it too difficult to live in Colombia, though he continues to go there and keeps in touch constantly. He is much too famous there, and of course certain sectors among the powerful are suspicious or openly hostile about his activities. In Bogotá in 1981 he found out he was about to be arrested and questioned about the revolutionary group M19, and he asked the Mexican government for asylum and safeconduct. With the money he was awarded in 1982 he established a new publication, *El otro*, an alternative press. Opposition was overwhelming and the paper didn't survive; it is perhaps his best-known failure.

He continues to write both journalism and fiction, to travel frequently, to keep in touch with his old friends—exclusively by telephone since he found out someone had sold some of his letters to a North American university. He continues trying to improve the situation in Latin America, disheartening enough to discourage just about anyone, and supporting the efforts of Contadora, a group of Central American national leaders, to avoid war in that area. His newest novel is also his longest. *El amor en los tiempos del Cólera (Love in the Time of Cholera)* of 1985 is in fact a love saga that lasts a good many years as well as pages, his first book done with a computer.

One Hundred Years of Solitude came out of a long literary tradition in Latin America beginning with the fabulous and unbelievable: the Spanish conquistadors already had visions of monsters, mermaids, and Amazons in their heads when they came to the New World. They were at once filled with awe, credulous, willing to believe in the fountain of youth, El Dorado, and the seven cities of gold, and in fact the power of suggestion, or expectation, must explain some of the wild and imaginative accounts of their voyages. The earliest Latin American literature is made up of letters and chronicles, true accounts of explorations and battles, all manner of legal documents, with some inevitable embellishment and exaggeration. During the colonial period most writers were more influenced by the literature of the fatherland than their own surroundings, especially since the period coincides with the Golden Age of Spanish literature. Other European trends were followed in the nineteenth century, especially the French literary masters, and it was not until very late in the century that a Latin American finally influenced Europeans. Nicaraguan Rubén Darío initiated the poetic period known as modernism, and was admired and imitated by Spanish and French poets.

In Colombia the romantic novel *María*, by Jorge Isaacs (1867), was one of the few works to be read outside the country, and indeed is still studied by pupils in many places in Latin America. The very realistic *La Vorágine (The Vortex)*, by José Eustasio Rivera, came out in 1924, and is a cornerstone of realism for all of Latin America. After the realism movement came a group of young writers who rebelled against the purely descriptive mode and felt that invention was at least as worthy as reflection. Several extremely important novels appeared in the 1940s, precursors of what has become known as "el boom," among them *el Señor Presidente (The President)*, by Nobel Prize winner Guatemalan Miguel Angel Asturias; *Al filo del agua (At the Edge of the Storm)*, by Mexican Agustín Yánez; and *El reino de este mundo (The Kingdom of This World)*, by the Cuban Alejo Carpentier. The influence of modern novelists from Europe and the United States can be seen in this work; Proust, Joyce, Dos Passos, Woolf, and Faulkner were well known among Latin American intellectuals of the period.

This refreshing trend continued in the 50s and 60s and gained momentum. Carpentier's masterpiece, *Los pasos perdidos (The Lost Steps)*, appeared in 1953; Lydia Cabrera's *El monte (The Hill)* in 1954; Juan Rulfo's brief but masterful *Pedro Páramo* in 1955; Carlos Fuentes's *La región más transparente (Where the Air Is Clear)* in 1985; Julio Cortázar's experimental *Rayuela (Hopscotch)* in 1963; Mario Vargas Llosa's *La casa verde (The Green House)* in 1965; Guillermo Cabrera Infante's *Tres tristes tigres (Three Trapped Tigers)* in 1967; and Manuel Puig's *La traición de Rita Hayworth (Betrayed by Rita Hayworth)* in 1968, to name a few. Though fewer new names appeared in the 70s, some did, and all those writers continued their work, some prolifically, into the 1980s. In 1982 a new masterpiece appeared: *La casa de los espíritus (The House of the Spirits)*, by Isabel Allende of Chile, followed by *De amor y de sombre (Of Love and Shadow)* in 1984 and *Eva Luna* in 1987 by the same author.

Even without *One Hundred Years of Solitude*, by far the most successful work of "el boom," the amount and quality of prose coming from Latin America in the last few decades is astonishing. Perhaps it's not possible to define and analyze all the factors that, juxtaposed, led to this great flowering of the novel in this particular time and place; the best news of all is that it doesn't show any sign of wearing out, or wearing thin, so far.

NOTES

1. Figures for casualties are very difficult to verify; this estimate is quoted by Oscar Collazos in *García Márquez: la soledad y la gloria* (Barcelona: Plaza y Janés, 1986) 26. See also Stephen Minta, *Gabriel García Márquez: Writer of Colombia* (London: Jonathan Cape, 1987) for a lucid discussion of the historical accounts. There is also some confusion about the date of Gaitán's assassination; a look at newspaper accounts verifies 1948.

2. Angel Flores claims the correct birth date is 1927, based on a conversation with García Márquez's father, in *Narrativa Hispanoamericana 1816–1981: Historia y antología* (Mexico: Siglo XXI, 1982) 4:429. Most sources claim 1928.

3. Like all human beings, Gabriel García Márquez sometimes exaggerates and sometimes contradicts himself. In this quotation, however, he is consistent and has repeated himself, and has been cited by nearly everyone who has written about him. One of the best sources for García Márquez on himself is the long interview he did with his friend Plinio Apuleyo Mendoza, *El olor de la guayaba (The Fragrance of the Guava)*; Bogotá: Oveja Negra, 1982.

4. García Márquez discusses this episode in his interview with Mendoza, and Graham Greene devoted a book to it: *Getting to Know the General: The Story of an Involvement* (New York: Simon and Schuster, 1984).

CHAPTER ONE

One Hundred Years of Solitude

On a narrow scale *One Hundred Years of Solitude* is the story, covering one hundred years and six generations, of the Buendía family and the founding of Macondo. Seen from a wider perspective it represents many other things as well;—the history of Colombia and of Latin America; even of humanity, from genesis to apocalypse.

How García Márquez is able to manage such a colossal undertaking has been the subject of thousands of pages of literary criticism and a good many interviews with the author. The number of themes encompassed in the novel is one explanation for its wholeness;—universal themes such as time and repetition, myth, love and sex, solitude, the search for knowledge and truth, writing and literature, to name a few. Within these broad categories are more specific ones: from love and sex to incest, with all its ramifications; from the search for knowledge to esoteric kinds of knowledge, such as alchemy and clairvoyance, as well as an exploration of writing systems and references to other literary works; from repetition to twins and images based on mirrors and reflections. Amazingly, those seemingly disparate and varied subjects form a unity, coming together like clockwork, for the novel is a closed system whose end begins with the first page.

García Márquez has said that every line in this work is based on reality. At first glance that might seem preposterous: yellow butterflies constantly flitting around a mechanic/lover; a line of blood that winds its way through town to find the mother of the victim; a young woman being assumed into heaven wrapped in expensive sheets; a man who disappears and another who returns from the dead. *One Hundred Years of Solitude* is fiction, imaginative, and best taken with a willing suspension of disbelief; above all, the novel is a search for truth, and its author uses all the resources available to him, including nontraditional, nonrational forms of knowledge usually discounted in our overly technological and superrational societies. As far as exaggeration is concerned, a glance at the newspapers will confirm the cliché that truth is stranger than fiction, and this novel gives us many points of departure to explore this folk wisdom.

As a way of approaching the novel, then, we can examine its major themes, how the author handles them, how he creates a reality, both magic and marvelous, within the world of Macondo. At the same time we can compare that creation with our own versions of reality, what we perceive through our senses, not leaving out the world as presented to us by the usual means of communication and mass media.

One Hundred Years of Solitude is technically a traditional novel in that its omniscient narrator dominates all aspects of the story. Although the action is not chronological, it has the function of evoking the end of a vital cycle from its beginning, so that the present is seen from the perspective of the past, a projection the future will give it. In the first sentence the narrator seems to be in the same time frame as the Colonel at the firing squad: "Many years later, as he faced the firing squad, Colonel Aureliano Buendía was to remember that distant afternoon when his father took him to discover ice."[1] But the firing sqad episode is a point of departure to describe the early days of Macondo, and it is not until the end of the chapter that the narrator returns to the ice, and many chapters after that to the firing squad. Throughout the novel the narration is in a closed time, with a beginning and an end; and all of whose "times," present, past, and future, can be recounted at any time by the narrator, who is equidistant from them all. The novel is made up of episodes that revolve on themselves, like a serpent biting its tail; the unnumbered chapters are made up of pieces of stories that create a spiral in time. Chapter after chapter begins with a startling statement, which is unraveled and explained in the most matter-of-fact terms, and ends where it started, having been explained so logically that no other conclusion to it seems possible. García Márquez uses constantly shifting verb tenses to create a spiral sensation, as in the opening sentence: the colonel "was to remember" an event from his childhood at some future point in time.

García Márquez's manipulation of time and creation of a closed, all-encompassing system within the book forces the reader to doubt the usual linear conception and measurement of time, and in fact calls into question the very time of the book itself. For if Melquíades's parchments are a history of the family, they are also its prophecy;

they predate the actions they describe. Melquíades is seen at intervals working on them, but more often giving certain members of the family clues to their interpretation. Time doubles over on itself as the last Aureliano is finally able to interpret and understand what is written; his reading of the manuscripts exists within the manuscripts he is reading, as he realizes he will not leave the room in which he is finally able to understand the parchments.

There are several points of comparison between Melquíades's creation and that of García Márquez. The wise gypsy "had not put events in the order of man's conventional time, but had concentrated a century of daily episodes in such a way that they coexisted in one instant" (382). Within the structure of *One Hundred Years of Solitude* the author does the same thing. Fragments of episodes run through several chapters and close in on themselves only after the intromission of several other episodes, which will close in their turn after having introduced others, and so on, such as the Amaranta/Pietro Crespi/Rebeca relationships. Just as Melquíades's story/ history seems to preexist his putting it down on the parchments—which he does not all at once but little by little, with long intervals in time and space in between— so can we see fragments of *One Hundred Years of Solitude* previous to its appearance in print. The author has said that he had the embryo for this novel in his head since his youth, and a look at several stories written earlier attest to that fact, notably *No One Writes to the Colonel* and *Leaf Storm*. An earlier title for the book might have been *La casa* (The House), based, as the au-

21

thor tells us, on the house of his grandparents, where he spent his earliest years.

To break our traditional conception of time García Márquez suggests the possibility of nonlinear time, that is, circular, cyclical, or spiraled. One of his most salient and obvious techniques, aside from fragmentation, is repetition. The names of the characters require a diagram of the family tree to avoid confusion, and along with the names certain characteristics are repeated, broken only in the case of the twins, José Arcadio Segundo and Aureliano Segundo, whose identity is suspect in any case because of the switching they did as children. The involvement of Pilar Ternera in successive generations of the family is so repetitive that at one point she fears incest and finds another woman, Santa Sofía de la Piedad, to satisfy the amorous desires of her son Arcadio.

It is time's refusal to move on that drives José Arcadio Buendía to madness, as he seeks some evidence that it is linear, as everyone believes. His positivistic mind will not allow him to believe anything he cannot "prove," and so when he seeks proof that Tuesday is different from Monday, and Wednesday from Tuesday, he gets stuck—not so much in time, as he believes, as in the vacuum between his failure to prove that basic assumption and his inability to imagine, or accept, other possibilities. Ursula comes to a similar conclusion later, expressed differently. When José Arcadio Segundo, in his inventive phase, wants to make a port of Macondo by digging a channel from the sea, she is so reminded of José Arcadio's harebrained schemes that she reacts in frustration: " 'I know all of this by heart,' Ursula would shout. 'It's as if time had turned around and we were back at the beginning' "

(185). Pilar Ternera, Ursula's counterpart in many ways, sees the cycles as revolving around an axle:

> There was no mystery in the heart of a Buendía that was impenetrable for her because a century of cards and experience had taught her that the history of the family was a machine with unavoidable repetitions, a turning wheel that would have gone on spilling into eternity were it not for the progressive and irremediable wearing of the axle (364).

Perhaps the image of an axle is the most appropriate, since the motion is seemingly progressing in one direction but in fact moves back continually to where it started. In this way we can accept that Pilar Ternera's function during the insomnia plague is to read the past, rather than the future, in her cards. An earlier similar image returns us to José Arcadio's prelude to madness. He becomes interested in Pietro Crespi's mechanical toys and synchronizes all the clocks to strike at the same moment and set off the dancing of a miniature ballerina. Other turns of the phrase, interspersed throughout the narration, jolt our usual concept of time as well: Fernanda is described as a widow whose husband hasn't died yet; Remedios is a fourteen-year-old great-grandmother, Ursula a newborn old lady; and when Aureliano goes to war, he has limited immortality. Using more conventional expressions of time profusely but usually not concretely, such as "much later," "many hours," "several years," "several centuries later," García Márquez evokes a kind of imprecise, legendary time. When he is specific about time, as when the rain is described as lasting four years, eleven months, and two days, the exactness startles us as much as the duration.

Another kind of circularity is seen in the family's hereditary vice of making things to unmake them: specifically, the Colonel's little gold fishes, sold for coins to be made into more fishes, and Amaranta's Penelope-like weaving of her shroud. Amaranta Ursula, like a parody of Ursula, always manages to keep busy, but the problems she resolves are of her own making; she does a poor job on a thousand things so she will have something to fix the next day.

Ursula's repetitions startle even herself. She discovers José Arcadio Segundo, forgotten years before in the secret room, his teeth covered with green slime and his eyes motionless. When she laments that he lives like a pig after all the trouble of teaching him good manners, he responds: " 'What did you expect?... Time passes.' " Ursula's response is exactly the same as Colonel Aureliano's when she visited him years before in his death cell: " 'That's how it goes,... but not so much' " (310). The words are out of her mouth before she realizes the repetition, which furnishes her with further evidence of what she already knows: time was not passing, as she had just said, but turning in a circle. But her age and loss of memory keep her from seeing a similar repetition, generational once again, and not at all uncommon, when she sees the youngest Aureliano. In spite of having seen him many times she asks him who he is:

" 'I'm Aureliano Buendía,' " he said.

" 'That's right,' " she replied. " 'And now it's time for you to start learning how to be a silversmith.' " She had confused him with her son again" (314).

In one last example of the manipulation of time García Márquez has an interesting literary precedent. When the

José Arcadio who would be pope but is actually more interested in his equivocal pleasures brings his young companions into the house, they become curious about their host's wild relative, Aureliano, who does nothing but work on the parchments. At one point when he is in the kitchen for a moment, four of them go into the laboratory to destroy the parchments, but as soon as they lay their hands on them, an "angelic force lifted them off the ground and held them suspended in the air until Aureliano returned" (342). Indeed, the suspension is in time as well as in space, and it recalls the miraculous suspension of the day on which Charlemagne's troops fight the Saracens in the account related in the epic myth *La chanson de Roland*. The warriors need more time in the light of day and have God on their side; the parchments need protection from the mischievous children and have an angelic force on their side.

Einstein's formulation of the theory of relativity led him to the conclusion that time itself is relative and has no absolute sense. Perhaps José Arcadio Segundo, considered mad by everyone, is envisioning the same concept: "he was the only one who had enough lucidity to sense the truth of the fact that time also stumbled and had accidents and could therefore splinter and leave an eternalized fragment in a room" (322).

For García Márquez, history and reality are as open to imaginative intrepretation as are time and memory, for if memory is known to be somewhat unreliable and our concept of time too rigid, so are many of our unquestioned assumptions. In a Jungian vision Aureliano sees Melquíades "like the materialization of a memory that had been in his head since long before he was born"

(328). It is the day he discovers that the manuscripts are written in Sanskrit, the prototype of modern Hindi as well as Romany, the language of the gypsies. It takes Fernanda longer to discover a reality she doesn't want to believe than it takes her to forget it: that Santa Sofía de la Piedad is her mother-in-law and not just some servant. This is an individual case of self-deception, but the novel contains examples of collective memory and its loss, which can lead to a false version of history, manipulated for political reasons. The banana company strike is a case in point.

For García Márquez's novelistic account of that historical episode, though the numbers might be somewhat inaccurate, is much closer to the truth than the official versions published after the event. In the novel the sleight-of-hand lawyers win their case by proving beyond all doubt that the workers never existed. At first glance this may seem an exaggeration typical of García Márquez. Historically, in fact, the company had often "proven" that its part-time workers didn't exist, in order to free themselves of the regulation, weak though it was, of organized labor. But an even greater feat of the company in the novel is the erasure from the collective memory of the people that the event had even occurred. The massacre has two survivors, José Arcadio Segundo and a small child. When José Arcadio returns to Macondo after the macabre train ride in one of many coaches filled with corpses, no one believes his version of what happened. During the endless downpour the officers in charge of exterminating union leaders tell the relatives of their victims that they must be dreaming if they thought something happened in Macondo. Sounding rather like

Voltaire's Candide, their standard reply is: "Nothing has ever happened, and nothing will ever happen. This is a happy town" (287).

The only person finally to believe the "mad" José Arcadio Segundo's version of the strike and massacre is the little Aureliano, years later. He, in his turn, is disbelieved when as an adult he leaves the house and tells his version to others. By now the obliteration of memory has gone a step further: the judicial documents and textbooks "prove" that the banana company never existed.

Although García Márquez's casualty figures are almost surely closer to the truth than the version of the officer in charge of the historical massacre, Cortés Vargas, who claimed there were nine, the author's representation of the facts is not concerned with accuracy in numbers. His version of the strike and its aftermath shows obvious sympathy with the strikers and aversion to the company, whose antics he treats with delicious irony. But his real concerns are, as always, related to a search for a larger truth. It is the historical conspiracy of silence that followed the strike that he sees as most dangerous. The Colombian government had nothing to gain and much to lose by letting out the facts of the case, and the witnesses were naturally reluctant to speak out in an aftermath of bloody reprisals. The episode, surely an extremely important one in the history of Colombia, is in danger of being lost or suppressed from the collective memory.

This leads to the question of most concern to García Márquez. How can "history" be given so much credit and be so unshakably believed when it is impossible to reconstruct? The eyewitness account of the historical event, by the officer in charge of the slaughter, is suspect, to say

the least. Newspaper accounts speak of the threat of bol-
shevism in the entire zone, and a telegram sent by the
U.S. Legation to the Secretary of State proudly announced that there were a thousand victims. The charis-
matic young lawyer Jorge Eliécer Gaitán did his own
unofficial investigation twenty years later and made of
the results a highly charged and emotional speech. He
was assassinated shortly afterward. García Márquez
makes no claim for accuracy in his figure of three thousand; in fact, he insists that this is not his point at all,
fully aware of the folly of seeking the truth in numbers
alone. The theme of reconstruction of a past event later
becomes a preoccupation, and indeed forms the basis for
the journalistic novella *Chronicle of a Death Foretold.*

Seen from a wider perspective this bloody episode represents the intervention of foreign, mostly American,
companies and their governments in Colombia in particular and Latin America in general. In Macondo, as important as the slaughter of workers is the effect the
banana company has on the town. The reader is often
given a historical perspective in the account of what happens in Macondo; founded by José Arcadio Buendía and
Ursula Iguarán, its beginnings are so primitive that
things don't have names and have to be pointed at. In
the tradition of a benevolent patriarch José Arcadio dis-
tributes land and access to water and shade. When he
becomes involved in his schemes and inventions, the
power vacuum is filled by Don Apolinar Moscote, who
represents one of the opposing sides in the dichotomy
that is Colombian politics, the liberals and the conservatives. Moscote is authoritarian and bureaucratic; more
interested in form than in substance, he orders all the

houses in the town to be painted blue, the color representing the conservatives. His son-in-law Aureliano becomes Colonel Aureliano when he sees the injustices committed by that party and joins the opposite one to start his endless series of civil wars. If he had a flash of idealism in his youth, he sees later that the fight is really about power. The two sides have in common that they represent the oligarchy and see that the development of foreign companies needs a few collaborators, historically not hard to find among the ruling classes. And so the banana company, with its official protection, comes, bringing with it sudden prosperity and modernization. When the workers revolt, its scientists begin an unnatural downpour which is the beginning of the ruin of the town, unable to recover from the disappearance of its newfound wealth. A dependency has been created, and the withdrawal of the company, with the rain as an excuse, leaves the town not only poor, as it was before, but weak and decadent. The end is near.

Some figures on the rise of banana production in the zone might be useful to bring this situation into perspective. United Fruit Company began operations at the turn of the century and by the 1930s controlled 60 percent of the banana trade world wide. It owned three-quarters of the banana-producing land in the province of Magdalena by 1938 and controlled much of the train system in Colombia, so that noncompany fruit could not be shipped. For a period of eight years it paid no export taxes. The peak years were the 1920s, when increasing construction caused a labor shortage, which in turn resulted in a certain labor militancy. But the laborers were no match for the powers against them, and the sad results of their struggles form a pattern constantly repeated in other Latin American countries as well.

To trace the historical perspective in *One Hundred Years of Solitude* back to its roots, one must begin, as does the history of Macondo, in times even earlier than the founding of the town. The novel is replete with historical references to Colombia's colonial past; thus a figure such as Sir Francis Drake takes on an importance in the novel that surpasses his contribution to the development of the northern area of Colombia. Melquíades links the name of the German explorer Alexander von Humboldt to the word *equinox* and to his own discovery of immortality.[2] But in García Márquez's efforts to recover lost history perhaps the most interesting case in point is his portrayal of the role of the Indians. Given the colonial situation and the efforts to annihilate the Indians, one is not surprised to see two Indians of royal blood as servants in the Buendía household, nor is it strange that they should be repeatedly associated with memory and its loss, both personally and collectively.

Documentation about the brutal massacres of Indians by Spanish conquerors is not hard to find, beginning with the Spanish priest Bartolomé de Las Casas, who is credited with giving the English ammunition aplenty to begin the *Leyenda negra,* the Black Legend.[3] Las Casas's efforts to restrain the violence of the soldiers were of little avail; as Columbus foresaw in his earliest letters to the King and Queen of Spain, their population had been decimated within thirty years. Perhaps Columbus realized that efforts to stop the brutality were doomed, or perhaps he was indifferent to their fate; in any case, his reaction was to try to save their existence from annihilation from the minds of men in a way that foreshadows García Márquez's efforts at recuperating lost history. On his second voyage he brought along a Catalan priest, Fray Ramón Pané, to record all he could about the customs and language of the Taino Indians of the island of Hispaniola, now the Dominican Republic and Haiti. This little book, surviving only in Italian translation, is our sole source of information about those unfortunate people, whose extermination took only a few decades.[4]

The myths and chronicles of the discovery of the New World are astonishing in volume and variety as well as in content. The documentation includes letters, legal papers of all sorts, eyewitness accounts, and chronicles based at times more on the expectations of the writers than on evidence of the senses. It is perhaps this combination of Old World mythology and a wonder at the awesome sights seen on the new continent that most captures our imagination. But the silenced history of Latin American is that of the vanquished, its pre-Columbian inhabitants.

The task of recovering lost history through writing once again links Melquíades to the author himself. The insomnia plague, brought to the town by Cataure and Visitación, first manifests itself in eternal vigilance but soon becomes a loss of memory. The Colonel, working in his silversmith laboratory, will make an effort to remember the names of things and their functions by labeling them; this painstaking task slows down the process of forgetting but is doomed to failure. It is Melquíades who brings the cure to the disease. The Colonel is fulfilling his role as an Aureliano here as a precursor to the others, those with lucid minds who, through the searchings of successive generations, will finally interpret the manu-

31

scripts prepared by Melquíades. José Arcadio is the exception here, but as we have seen and will explore in some detail later, his identity as a José Arcadio is suspect. Similarly, the role of the author in this context can be seen as a rediscovery, a rewriting of an endangered history, just as an account by the Indians of the so-called discovery of the continent would present something quite different from the official story.

It is, in fact, Visitación who first becomes alarmed about the loss of memory she knows will come:

> She meant that when the sick person became used to this state of vigil, the recollection of his childhood began to be erased from his memory, then the name and notion of things, and finally the identity of people and even the awareness of his own being, until he sank into a kind of idiocy that had no past (50).

In an interesting repetition of this syndrome, the deluge of nearly five years produces "an indolence of the people ... in contrast to the voracity of oblivion, which little by little was undermining memories in a pitiless way" (318). It is on the occasion of another anniversary, that of the Treaty of Neerlandia, when some emissaries come to Macondo to honor descendants of the Colonel, who himself had rejected those honors several times. The gypsies also return around that time, and they find such a state of forgetfulness and defeat that they repeat the activities of their ancestors for the descendants of the first inhabitants of Macondo: once again they bring in their magnets, magnifying glasses, and false teeth in a pattern that is repeated throughout the book in small incidents and by the book as a whole. Toward the novel's close, while the final couple is making love out of love, a different manifestation of memories invades the house, echoing the ghosts of the house of the author's grandparents:

> They could hear Ursula fighting against the laws of creation to maintain the line and José Arcadio Buendía searching for the mythical truth of the great inventions, and Fernanda praying, and Colonel Aureliano Buendía stupefying himself with the deception of war and the little gold fishes, and Aureliano Segundo dying of solitude in the turmoil of his debauches (378).

The presence of these ancestral inhabitants gives the lovers joy, for they realize that as apparitions they will continue to live after death.

In a different sort of character those inherited memories can bring fear and paralysis. While Ursula is training José Arcadio to be pope, she is also teaching him all her frustrations and disillusionments. He becomes afraid not only of tattletale saints, with whom he is threatened, but of everything:

> . . .women on the street, who would ruin his blood; the women in the house, who bore children with the tail of a pig; fighting cocks, who brought on the death of men and remorse for the rest of one's life; firearms, which with a mere touch would bring down twenty years of war; uncertain ventures, which led only to disillusionment and madness (340).

Only his fantasies/memories of Amaranta give him some relief from this transmitted terror; both the torment and a release from it are experiences once removed.

The question of rediscovery, rather than discovery, is

present from the opening of the novel and has the function of undercutting assumptions throughout. José Arcadio, looking for a passage to the sea, as had generations of explorers on the continent, finds a fifteenth-century suit of armor and a Spanish galleon left behind by those ancestors. The knowledge brought to Macondo by the gypsies is ancient; it is not new but forgotten, such as the ancient Greek technique of setting enemy ships aflame by concentrating the sun's rays through glass. The patriarch's own scientific experiments are "discoveries" found years or centuries before by others. His work is not undervalued for its lack of originality; on the contrary, Melquíades rewards him with an alchemist's laboratory when he discovers that the earth is round. For a colonial inhabitant of the New World to make this discovery is on the one hand a result of the loss of memory of those who went before him; it is also a delicious irony on the "discovery" of the New World itself, called in Latin America with a sad appropriateness *El día de la raza* (The Day of Our Race).

In a final example of an ironic distortion of history caused by failed memory, and underscoring the importance of names or labels, the ancient Father Nicanor Reyna asks the last Aureliano, who is madly searching through the church archives for clues to his identity, what his name is. Hearing "Aureliano Buendía," the priest links it not to any of his ancestors, but to a street named after them: "Many years ago there used to be a street here with that name and in those days people had the custom of naming their children after streets" (376).

Memory can easily be lost and history distorted; but there are other forms of knowledge which have been sup-

34

pressed by our rationalist culture and which seem to have captured the attention of García Márquez for their rich possibilities. The gypsies bring alchemy to Macondo along with their technological wonders. Melquíades, an honest man, warns José Arcadio that the magnets his tribe brings to Macondo won't work for extracting gold from the ground. José Arcadio sees this as the most important end; just as his conquistador forebears had done, he abuses the powers he is offered to attain this goal. His attempts at alchemy are impure and doomed to failure for this reason: the alchemist's quest is for inner knowledge and spiritual wholeness, his purification being represented by the transformation of base metal into gold. The creation of the precious metal is to be sought for its symbolism, not for its market value. José Arcadio's failure is even worse; not only is he unable to "create" gold, but the gold he starts with becomes impure as he mixes it with other, baser metals. Similarly, the Spanish colonizers melted down religious objects for their gold, a great deal of which was later lost in the oceans.

The symbolism of alchemy runs beyond Melquíades's gift to José Arcadio. Ursula is scandalized by evidence of her own paganism when she discovers that the statue of Saint Joseph she has been praying to for years is filled with gold and therefore she has been worshiping gold. Aureliano wears himself out looking for the treasure, but it is not to be found until years later, by the young companions of José Arcadio, returned from Rome. Wandering around the dark house one night, "they saw a yellow glow coming through the crumbling cement, as if an underground sun had changed the floor of the room into a pane of glass" (342). In this multiple image we have not

35

only the gold itself, but also the sun, accompanied by the transformation of the decaying floor into a glowing pane of glass.

Other forms of nonrational knowledge are important to Macondo's development. If Pilar Ternera's readings of the cards are supplemented by her experience, the many prophecies of various kinds stand on their own. The Colonel was acknowledged as clairvoyant since his birth with his eyes open, and indeed his prophecies are accurate, if not particularly useful. Ursula is unaware that she is predicting the family's fate—just as Melquíades's parchments are to do—when, after the rains, she begins a renewed period of feverish activity: " 'A person can't live in neglect like this,' she said. 'If we go on like this we'll be devoured by animals' " (309).

At times the "false" knowledge in Macondo is the result of an inappropriate blend of different kinds of wisdom or an improper use of the tools of knowledge. Just as José Arcadio substituted some of the ingredients in the alchemist's laboratory, dooming the process to failure, he uses concrete modern technology to prove abstractions: he refuses to believe in God unless he can capture an image of him with his daguerreotype. The technology of the movies enchants the people from the town until they become aware of its fiction, or rather its lack of literalness. When an actor whose death they lament in one film reappears safe and sound in the next, they destroy the theater.

Madness, too, may be seen in the novel as a form of knowledge unperceived by the sane. When José Arcadio can't accept the nonpassage of time, he shouts a gibberish incomprehensible to the townspeople. Later, when he

36

is the only one to understand the priest's levitation, we realize along with the priest that the gibberish is Latin; he has attained not only the ancient language but its logic as well. Other characters seem extraordinarily lucid in their presumed madness: Remedios the Beauty is considered insane for not wishing to wear clothing in a tropical climate; the Colonel tries to isolate himself from others by drawing a circle around himself, having been the target of attempted assassinations. In the case of José Arcadio Segundo, a loss of contact with everyday reality follows the banana company massacre and the denial by everyone of something he witnessed himself. García Márquez has scientific as well as literary precedents for his views on madness. British psychiatrist R.D. Laing believed that to function normally in our insane society, one must be mad, and Andrew Weil thought that seeking to change modes of perception is a basic human need.[5] Nothing could be more logical, indeed, given the injustices in the world, than to try, as Don Quixote did, to right wrongs and help people in distress.

The last Aureliano's final success in deciphering the manuscripts is a result of his putting together the different kinds of knowledge. Melquíades coaches him, as he had done during earlier attempts, and, represents the several forms of non-rational knowledge plus his ancient traditional language, Sanskrit. But he also guides Aureliano into the bookshop of the wise Catalonian, whose lively and close-set blue eyes "had the gentleness of a man who had read all of the books" (338). Aureliano reads the encyclopedia as if it were a novel, and learns Sanskrit in the process. But as the pope's apprentice realizes, Aureliano knows things that aren't in the encylopedia. To his surprised queries, Aureliano replies only that everything is known, suggesting that all discoveries are really rediscoveries and that real wisdom lies in deciphering what already exists.

The opposition between knowledge represented by rational and classical sources and that of secret, intuitive sources is echoed in many themes, characters, and symbols in the novel, including the symbolism of alchemy, made up of such dualities as sun/moon and gold/silver. Among the most significant are those that combine to create: man/woman in engendering and blue/red elements resulting in the purple of the philosopher's stone. The blending of the Sanskrit and Latin traditions is represented by Melquíades and the wise Catalonian in a search for knowledge. The opposition of characters underscores the dual nature of reality, most obvious in the binary set of José Arcadios and Aurelianos. Ursula concludes that except for the twins, "while the Aurelianos were withdrawn, but with lucid minds, the José Arcadios were impulsive and enterprising, but they were marked with a tragic sign" (174). Among the women there are good women and bad women in the traditional sense: Ursula the virtuous mother, Pilar the sinful mother; Fernanda the virtuous wife, Petra the fecund lifetime companion; Amaranta the family member and virgin, Rebeca the outsider and unaccepted wife of José Arcadio. In ideas there is an opposition as well; we have seen the undermining of the linear concept of time by the suggestion of a circular or cyclical pattern, reinforced by the structure of the novel itself. Politically, the liberals and conservatives seem different to Colonel Aureliano in the beginning, but seen with some experience they represent two sides of a coin, as some would say of our Republicans and Democrats. Emotionally, the thin line that separates love from hate is best seen in the care with which Amaranta plans her revenge against Rebeca. So carefully is it drawn that "she would have carried [it] out in exactly the same way if it had been done out of love, but she would not allow herself to become upset by the confusion" (259).

The oppositions in *One Hundred Years of Solitude* function structurally within the novel to reinforce its circularity, just as the back-and-forth movement of a pendulum really forms an arc, a section of a circle. The most interesting case, for the sameness of the two members and for its startling basis in reality, is that of the twins. José Arcadio Segundo and Aureliano Segundo are so alike as children that to avoid confusion they are dressed in color-coded clothing and name bracelets. They frustrate these efforts by switching, and indeed Ursula becomes convinced that they have traded identities permanently. This would account for their characteristics not matching those of their many namesake predecessors, and is confirmed when they are accidentally buried in each other's graves by Aureliano Segundo's drunken friends.

The mirror-image depiction of the twins reinforces García Márquez's brilliant use of reflections, mirrors, and mirages, which culminates in the final episode, where Aureliano reads of himself reading the parchments "as if he were looking into a speaking mirror" (383). Reflections are fluid, visions can be mirages, and images can be mistakenly interpreted, just as José Arcadio's dream of a city of ice turns out to be a city of mirrors or mirages. As small children the twins take advantage of their similarity to perform a mirror-image ritual, one performing with the left hand what the other does with the right, in identical gestures. But differences develop in late adolescence. A decisive incident occurs when an execution by firing squad is scheduled in Macondo; José Arcadio Segundo begs to be allowed to see it, while Aureliano Segundo is horrified at the thought. In an episode that foreshadows his witnessing of the slaughter of strikers, José Arcadio Segundo is to be haunted forever by the vision of the condemned man, felled by the rifles but with his eyes still open, and by the belief that this man was buried alive. Aureliano, on the other hand, begins to take an interest in the parchments.

They are still enough alike to fool Petra Cotes, who believes she is making love with a tireless José Arcadio Segundo but in fact is satisfying both twins. This encounter marks the beginning of very different life styles; José Arcadio loses interest, but Aureliano begins with her a life of unparalleled debauchery. Petra receives credit for the extraordinary fertility of his animals, which makes him a rich man, all the more able to enjoy his debauchery, adding to his wealth in an upward spiral that would delight capitalists and epicureans alike. He becomes fat and sluggish, while José Arcadio begins to take an interest in inventions, as his great-grandfather had done, and in politics, as the Colonel had done. After the strike and his apparent madness, no one needs to tie him to a chestnut tree, for he locks himself up in Melquíades's room, a space for him with a dual role: while it protects him from the police with its magical qualities, it presents to him the parchments to study so that he can begin his foreordained task of classifying their symbols. These two aspects of the room are borne out later when he fulfills his role as transmitter of knowledge to the last Aureliano: he convinces him of his version of the banana company strike and teaches him what he has learned about the deciphering of the parchments.

The fluid, changing characteristics of the twins are an exception to the pattern of namesakes. José Arcadio Segundo's brief tinkering with crazy inventions and schemes is consistent with his name, but his interest in politics belongs more properly to the Aurelianos. Aureliano Segundo's debauchery reminds Ursula so much of her son José Arcadio that she thinks the twins have inherited all the faults of the family and none of the strengths. All the Buendías suffer from the solitude of the novel's title, but generally it is the Aurelianos who shut themselves up in the laboratory. Ursula makes this diagnosis in a moment of despair; in fact, the twins seem to have all the characteristics of the male members of the family. The dedication of the patriarch can be seen in José Arcadio Segundo when he tries to decode the mysterious parchments, and later in the Aureliano who is destined to succeed. The excesses of the second José Arcadio when he returns from his life with the gypsies are echoed in Aureliano Segundo and later repeated by his son José Arcadio's erotic baths with young children. The intelligence and lucidity which make the original José Arcadio the leader in Macondo develop in José Arcadio Segundo and are passed on to the last Aureliano.

During the period of the endless rains Aureliano Segundo returns to his house, leaves his debauchery behind, and begins a period of activity. He loses weight, and as they grow old, the twins begin to resemble each other once again. They die at exactly the same moment, José Arcadio on the parchments, and Santa Sofía de la Piedad keeps her promise to slit his throat so he won't be buried alive. Aureliano succumbs to his excruciating throat ailment, described as steel crabs eating his throat away.

Since García Márquez claims everything he has written has a starting point in reality, a look at real-life twins might be instructive. There are so many cases of identical twins sharing an apparent biological clock that the incident of simultaneous death is neither fantasy nor exaggeration. A sensational case occurred in New York when twin gynecologists, both heavy drug users, were found dead in one of their apartments, both having died at the same time of withdrawal symptoms. Just before Christmas in 1979 elderly twin sisters were found dead in their New Jersey home. Giving birth can be quite as simultaneous; twin sisters married to twin brothers in Dallas, Texas, gave birth to their first child within minutes of each other in 1987. There are many examples of similar characteristics, telepathy, extremely strong bonding, special linguistic development, crises and mix-ups of identity, and shared pain of twins.[6] Recent research suggests that twins reared apart are more alike than twins raised together, which some believe results from an effort to be different on the part of twins who are constantly being compared and whose individuality is threatened by the presence of a double.

The constantly shifting relationships between reality; the imagination; and the sources of information in the novel have been commented on by García Márquez him-

42

self. Since the appearance of his novel he has been sent information such as the finding of an abandoned ship in the middle of the jungle and the revelation by a man of Barranquilla that he has something more than other men: the tail of a pig.

Parallel to the narration of extraordinary events that turn out to be true, the author presents the reader with a number of normal events related as if they were quite out of the ordinary: the discovery of ice and magnets, the tinkering with early technological devices. The result is an expansion of the concept of reality on the part of the reader; if we are to widen our horizons, we must go beyond what the appearances of things tell us, he seems to be saying. Within the novel the characters display very different ideas of reality and reactions to its challenge: Ursula, the practical one, covers her ears with wax when the birds sing so she won't lose her sense of reality. Her husband, the dreamer, is fascinated by an immediate reality that goes beyond his fertile imagination, an attitude and experience he shared with some of the conquistadors of the New World. Showing us the absurdity of the "proofs," for example, of Meme's willingness to enter the convent, and Mr. Jack Brown from Alabama's transformation into Dagoberto Fonseca of Macondo, the author creates a new version of reality, based on fragments of reality, like dreams or literature itself.

In addition to the historical details in *One Hundred Years of Solitude,* which are sometimes unspecific but nonetheless true in a general sense, the literary figures and incidents woven into the novel add another dimension to the tapestry of reality García Márquez has created. For along with figures based on the history of

Colombia, such as the Colonel, and on García Márquez's childhood memories, such as Amaranta, there are episodes and minor characters from previous literature, and even the citation of literary works themselves, such as José Zorrilla's *El puñal del godo,* a nineteenth-century play, transformed here into *The Dagger of the Fox* to fit the requirements of an absurd censorship. Aureliano's final interpretation of the family history represents a direct intervention within the novel of one of its characters, surely a reflection of certain characters in the second part of *Don Quixote* who have read the first part. The American machinations in Macondo resemble a peculiar combination of the idealism of that knight errant with the serviceable cynicism of another great figure of Spanish literature, Celestina, the protagonist of Fernando de Rojas's fifteenth-century novel in dialogue of the same name, in a sentence that reflects the language of the two works. On a glorious Wednesday morning the company "brought in a trainload of strange whores, Babylonish women skilled in age-old methods and in possession of all manner of unguents and devices to stimulate the unaroused, to give courage to the timid, to satiate the voracious, to exalt the modest man, to teach lessons to repeaters, and to correct solitary people" (214–15).

Latin American literary tradition is particularly present. The room smelling of boiled cauliflower which Gabriel rents in Paris is the one in which "Rocamadour was to die" (374). This tribute to Julio Cortázar's complex novel *Rayuela (Hopscotch)* is perhaps also reflected in the description of the coding Melquíades uses, the even lines in one ancient code and the odd ones in another. A Carlos Fuentes character actually appears in the pages of the novel as companion in arms to the Colonel, after having fought in the Mexican revolution: Colonel Lorenzo Galiván claims to have witessed the "heroism of his comrade Artemio Cruz" (278), another Fuentes protagonist who might still have been thought of as a hero at this point by that specific colonel, but is in fact one of the Mexican businessmen who became wealthy by making pacts with exploitative American companies. José Arcadio, in his wanderings with the gypsies, sees the pirate ship of Alejo Carpentier's Victor Hugues, looking for a route to Guadeloupe. Borges could certainly have inspired some of the endless reflections and symmetries in the novel, as well as Aureliano's final understanding, which has to be simultaneous with his death. In a much more general way, the novel's attempt to present an alternative version of Latin American history relates it to two long poems with the same function: Pablo Neruda's *Canto general* (General Song) and Octavio Paz's *Piedra de sol* (Stone of the Sun).

Most interesting is the author's use of characters out of his own previous writings. In the manner of the great nineteenth-century novelists, the Spaniard Benito Pérez Galdós and the Frenchman Honoré de Balzac, he weaves in characters from or references to his earlier stories. Grieving Amaranta Ursula's death but not yet aware of his own coming end, Aureliano recalls visions "he had contemplated with childish fascination from the courtyard of the curlews" (380), a reflection from the early story "La noche de los alcaravanes" ("The Night of the Curlews"). Big Mama's funeral carnival passes through the pages of the novel, as does the itinerant photographer who brushes with Eréndira and her heartless grandmother. Colonel Aureliano Buendía realizes that his soldiers will share the fate of that other colonel, who spends his life waiting for a pension that never comes, and Ursula, like that colonel, takes a lifetime of frustration to sum things up finally in a word: "Shit!" The technique is an interweaving of one more of the many forms of reality the author would like the reader to include in a reconstruction of reality.

Finally, the overwhelming themes of solitude, love, sex, and death are intimately related here. If the last fated couple in the novel are the only ones who conceive a child in love, many others experience something in between love and hate, as Rebeca and Amaranta or the last Aureliano and his strange uncle. Even the hatred of the original José Arcadio for Prudencio Aguilar becomes love through the solitude of death. Certainly the greatest part of the lovemaking is based on frustrations and taboos. The original pair abstain because of Ursula's fears of incest until they become the subject of gossip; the Colonel goes to Pilar Ternera for lack of Remedios; and Aureliano goes to Nigromanta before he finds solace with Amaranta Ursula.

Incest plays an important part, aside from its role in framing the entire family and narration, from Ursula's relation with José Arcadio to Aureliano's with Amaranta Ursula. The second José Arcadio is accused of incest when he marries Rebeca, and they are ostracized from the family, though strictly speaking they are not brother and sister. Amaranta's propensity for arousing amorous games in her young nephews leaves her technically a virgin and their desires perpetually unfulfilled. Colonel Aureliano's confusion between mother, wife, and daughter is increased by his misery as he prepares to face the firing squad:

> On another occasion, he felt at least a confused sense of shame when he found the smell of Ursula on his own skin, and more than once he felt her thoughts interfering with his. But all of that had been wiped out by the war. Even Remedios, his wife, at that moment was a hazy image of someone who might have been his daughter (167).

In another episode of the transposition of time, someone disturbs the solitude of the Colonel by asking him how he is feeling. He replies that he is waiting for his funeral procession to pass. Similarly, Amaranta foresees and announces her death long before it occurs, and prepares her shroud endlessly. She even offers to take letters to the dead, since she knows the exact hour of her own demise. Ursula, well over one hundred years old, nevertheless waits until the rains are over to take the step. All these prophetic visions of death form a repeated foreshadowing of the final episode, when Aureliano realizes he will not leave the room in which he is reading the parchments, for "races condemned to one hundred years of solitude did not have a second opportunity of earth" (383).

NOTES

1. *One Hundred Years of Solitude* (New York: Avon, 1970) 11. All quotations are from this edition; page numbers are noted parenthetically.

2. Humboldt spent the first five years of the nineteenth century in

northern Latin America; the book resulting from his explorations is entitled *Voyage aux régions équinoxiales du Nouveau Continent (1805)*.

3. Las Casas was a Dominican priest who lived and worked in Cuba, the Dominican Republic, and Mexico in the first half of the sixteenth century. A protector and defender of the Indians, he instigated the *Leyes Nuevas* (New Laws) in 1542 to protect them, but to little avail. His chilling accounts of the genocide of the Native Americans by Spaniards can be found in *Brevísima historia de la destrucción de las Indias,* first published in 1552.

4. Ramón Pané, *Relación acerca de las antigüedades de los indios,* ed. J. J. Arrom (Mexico: Siglo XXI, 1974).

5. See Ronald D. Laing, especially *The Politics of Experience* (New York: Ballantine, 1967), and Andrew Weil, *The Natural Mind* (Boston: Houghton Mifflin, 1972).

6. There are many studies of twins. Of particular interest are the results of a long and ongoing study by the University of Minnesota. Two cases of special linguistic development are those of Gracy and Ginny Kennedy in Columbus, Georgia, and those described in *Poto and Cabengo,* a 1979 film by Jean-Paul Gorin. For articles about identical twins reared apart, see *Science* (Mar. 1980): 23–28; *Psychology Today* (Jan. 1981): 58–80; and *Smithsonian,* (Oct. 1980): 48–57.

CHAPTER TWO

The Autumn of the Patriarch

Upon a first reading *The Autumn of the Patriarch* seems quite unlike its mythical predecessor. The first is a family chronicle told by an omniscient narrator, the second a study of the abject decadence of a senile dictator. And yet, within the innovative technique developed in this second novel we see the unmistakable hand of García Márquez, in style as well as in preoccupations—or, as Vargas Llosa so aptly called them in earlier works, "demons."[1] For while García Márquez describes the last years of the life of this nameless tyrant, he again explores themes he has dealt with earlier: the passage of time, the creation of myth, the loss or transformation of history, solitude, love, death, and meanings of reality itself. And although the style is new and experimental, the flow and rhythm as well as the ironic humor identify the author of *One Hundred Years of Solitude* beyond question.

When the author calls this novel a poem on the solitude of power, he at once points to its two major themes and, given the subject matter, to its surprising lyricism. Indeed, the focus is on definitions of power and apparent power, and as always some suggestions for other realities beyond the obvious. The protagonist of the novel is a composite figure made up of several dictators not confined to Latin America, and many of the anecdotes about his activities are based on fact, inspired by a battery of strongmen throughout the world. But while García Márquez relates episodes of absolutely godlike power on the part of the patriarch, he undermines that vision in a number of ways: the patriarch's helplessness vis-à-vis certain other forces, including the inevitable foreign powers; his inability to relate to other human beings, which leads inexorably to his abysmal solitude; and the vision of him as an old man and, in the circularity typical of the author, a man-child.

In the early sections he seems more than a god in his ability to control time and correct divine errors such as earthquakes, eclipses, and leap years. Blind people and lepers besiege him, asking for salt to cure their infirmities, just as they had accosted Jesus Christ. But these "miracles" are always undercut in some way; we do not see the cures but the besieging, and after all it is his adulators who proclaim all manner of bizarre, better-than-God titles for him. He "controls" time because he controls the people who tell him what time it is, and to his queries they answer, of course, "Whatever time you want, general sir." After his death these same shadowy adulators proclaim him general of the universe.

The question of the source of his power is complex. Obviously his incredible, ruthless brutality is a sine qua non, but it takes more than this sole ingredient to control a country. García Márquez points to the collaboration of many people, and most especially to the debilitating habit of passively being governed. When the plural narrators find the corpse, they are afraid to believe he is really dead, not only because they have heard of previous deaths that were not deaths, but also because an existence without him is unimaginable to them, no matter how hated he was. The fishwife, for example, breaks into sobs, saying, "my God, what's going to become of us without him."[2] The mythicizing of his power makes him

> invulnerable to plague and invulnerable to time, dedicated to the messianic happiness of thinking for us, knowing that we knew that he would not take any decision for us that did not have our measure, for he had not survived everything because of his inconceivable courage or his infinite prudence but because he was the only one among us who knew the real size of our destiny (99).

It is an attitude born of generations of repression and reinforced by more tangible sources of power, especially violence. The activities of his aides, Rodrigo de Aguilar and the Guajiro Indian Santos, are a mere prelude to the mass murderer Saenz de la Barra, who sends countless severed heads to the general like so many ripe coconuts, embodying the fatalistic idea that there's always another aspiring tyrant waiting in the wings who might be even worse. But underlying the most brutal description of the dictator's goons is something more terrifying. Those three righthand men are dispensable, but throughout the pages of *The Autumn of the Patriarch* we see the results of another faceless, nameless crew responsible for other massacres. The dynamiting of the ship loaded with two thousand children like the Biblical Holy Innocents is the beginning of the end for Aguilar, whose brutality is limited: he becomes pale at the news of the slaughter of the lottery ticket sellers. When Saenz becomes so violent that the dictator gets nervous, he is "disappeared" by still other faithful servants.

Political astuteness is one of the patriarch's major attributes. He must never give an order he is not sure will be carried out; he must be perceived as all powerful, and to do this he must continually rekindle and elaborate myths for public consumption. He also knows that when an enemy is created, that threat must be eliminated: no survivors. All the rebellious generals must die; Poncio Daza, whose new wife the general has just raped, must be cut up into "such thin slices that it was impossible to put his body back together again after it had been scattered by the hogs, poor man, but there was no other way out, he said, because he would have been a mortal enemy for the rest of his life" (94). The only person he kills himself is the card woman who showed him his future in the basins, for she had a kind of power he lacked.

His power to rule by decree is valid only as long as it is accepted by others; thus he proclaims that the gilt stone cathedral is the most beautiful in the world, and so be it. Much more commonplace, but just as farfetched, he changes time by silly artifice, and changes the dates of national holidays. Perhaps his greatest triumphs over nature are really just announcements: the bringing of the comet and the stopping of the hurricane. Or the manipulation of the perception of reality itself: "He put an end to all disagreement with the final argument that it didn't matter whether something back then was true or not, God damn it, it will be with time" (159); that is, he has the power to manipulate history.

Power is never far removed from money, and thus we see in the dictator a sad reflection of Latin American realities; in an inevitable spiral his funds and his power increase each other. No one dares to beat him at dominoes or cock fights; he taxes everything, including the waters of the nation and the right to walk in the shade. His scheme for always winning the lottery results in the slaughter of the two thousand children used to pick the tickets precisely because of their innocence. But his real sources of cash have to come from beyond the borders, and foreign interests are always ready to help him support the necessary armed forces to continue the stability of the regime. In an episode somewhat reminiscent of the late dictator Anastasio Somoza's appropriation of the worldwide help sent to Nicaragua after the disastrous earthquakes of 1972, the nation is rebuilt and armed forces restored

> since he had distributed the shipments of food and medicine and the material for public relief from foreign aid among the members of the high command, ever since the families of his ministers had Sunday outings at the beach with the Red Cross portable hospitals and field tents, they sold shipments of blood plasma, the tons of powdered milk to the ministry of health and the ministry of health resold them to charity hospitals (101)

and so on in a spiral of corruption that always enriches those within his framework of power.

Paradoxically the more powerful he becomes, the more vulnerable too, on various levels. If his rise to power is aided by foreign interests, he becomes indebted to them, and we finally see them measuring off the sea in sections to cart it off to Arizona. The thugs who help him suppress rebellions also hold sway over him, and nothing is

53

as pathetic as the dictator's resolve by night to rid himself of the bloodthirsty Saenz de la Barra, only to fall for his absurd but somehow convincing arguments the next day. The general's control over information in an earlier day becomes a way for his aides to control him, as we see him reading the one copy of a newspaper printed only for him, without knowing what is really going on. When they carelessly play a newsreel backward, he knows they are hiding something from him. His isolation is total, and he understandably trusts no one.

His relationship with the church is purely practical from the beginning: why should the church bother to convert him if he's doing just what they want anyway? The episode of the canonization of his mother culminates in the expulsion of all church people and expropriation of their lands. Just as Henry VIII initiated a kind of civil annulment when he couldn't get the church to support his desire to be rid of his wife, so the dictator throws out the church and proclaims civil sanctity for his mother, whose life was as pious as that of an unrepentant Magdalene. Ironically, the church will be restored and generously indemnified by another female figure who has power over the general, Leticia Nazareno.

As Leticia's power, based on her wild animal smell that so attracts the dictator, becomes so abusive that her life is in danger, the general realizes that he will not be able to protect her, even with "the ferocious escort of presidential guards under the instructions to kill without cause" (184). Her greed has pitted her against the privileges of the armed forces, and as the general knows so well, he is stronger than any one of them but not as

strong as any two plotting against him. And so,
and her son will be devoured by dogs.

No psychological study would be complete without a
dream, and the dictator has one which links his bloody
past with his present fears and results in the liquidation
of the senate and the supreme court, accomplished with
the indifference of the armed forces. As his minister of
health points out, the dream has already occurred in history; it is the story of the general's predecessor, General
Lautaro Muñoz, from whom he had wrested power. In
the dream the dictator's fear became relief as he was dying, but the terror returned with his awakening and "he
did nothing to disguise the terrible exorcism of the bad
dream but took advantage of the occasion to liquidate
the legislative and judicial apparatus of the old republic"
(89), precisely the "pale men in gray frock coats who
were smiling and sticking him with butcher knives" (87-
88) in the dream.

The general, defined over and over again as the most
solitary man on earth, a solitary drowned man and a
great solitary orphan, even finds himself "alone in the
people of his dreams" (61). García Márquez does not try
to establish a clear cause-effect relationship of power/
solitude, but rather depicts a spiral that can only end
with the dictator's death. If the patriarch's solitude
comes from his lack of ability to communicate with
others, then perhaps it leads to his need for power. Just
as he can't trust anyone as a result of his power, he cannot have human relationships because of his inability to
communicate. His sexuality symbolizes his power in the
macho tradition; he fathers five thousand children, but
the fecundity is undercut—they are all seven-month

runts. He is prolific but ineffective. Until he finds Leticia Nazareno his fornication is done quickly and badly, without taking off his clothes, "as if he had been older than he was, or much younger" (93). Such a fundamental need as love, then, is unattainable by this all-powerful supplanter of God. His perversion is symbolized by his herniated testicle, which emits a whistling sound during periods of acute tension. After the gruesome death of Leticia Nazareno, the only woman who could get him to take his clothes off to make love, his sexual interest turns to young girls. In a confusion of bodily functions which brilliantly symbolizes prostitution, he seems especially fond of inserting food into their vaginas, just as his mother had had to use her lower parts in order to eat.

Perhaps his exaggerated devotion to his mother is due to his suspicions of everyone else around him; in any case, Leticia Nazareno also becomes a mother figure for him, as she wacks his behind, scolds him for bad manners, and teaches him to read, using children's rhymes to do so. He is already in the state of regression that will see him as a helpless child at the end, wandering around in the dark corridors of his solitary palace. Even to his mother he seems at once older than herself and still a child. His power, solitude, and sexuality amount to a great masturbation: the solitary vice of power.

In his efforts to confuse others the patriarch ends up confusing himself, and in fact suffers a series of identity crises. If the narrators who enter the palace to find the body are unable to find "any trace of his life that could have led us to the unmistakable establishment of his identity" (83), it is because they have heard that there was a previous death, that of the dictator's perfect double, Patricio Aragonés. At first humiliated by the existence of the double, because it indicates a kind of equality, he then sees the usefulness of having the double appear in public for him, and finally he finds photographs of himself so old that he knows many of them are of Aragonés, whose name he can't remember. It is a prelude to not remembering who he himself is when death appears and calls him Nicanor. He has to tinkered with facts and perceptions, at the same time playing such contradictory roles over the years—patriarch to the people and devoted son to his mother, commander of everything within the country and puppet to foreign forces—that perhaps he has lost track of his own reality, which has sometimes been shaped more by those around him than by himself.

For as those plural narrators know, there is always another truth behind truth. García Márquez constantly pulls the rug out from under the false realities he sets up; even the animals' senses are confused as they nibble on the sections of the tapestries that depict wheat fields. The cows that inhabit the desolate palace are questionable too, even as they appear on the presidential balcony of an upstairs salon. The decor of the palace reflects the unreal, the illusory or the phony with its papier-mâché Doric capitals and Babylonic columns crowned with alabaster palm trees. His physical description, made up by the historians, is false as well; his clothing shows he was not huge, and in fact his clothes are seen as so baggy they don't seem to have anyone inside. His origins are doubtful; not the result of a virgin birth, as canonization efforts would have it; not the lack of male intervention, but the intervention of an unknown male, for his mother could never identify his father in the parade of men who passed through that musty back room where she earned her daily sustenance. Instead of one birth certificate he has three, as if to affirm an existence no one is sure about.

If the general's manipulations and tricks make all documentation suspect and even confuse him, the one reality he believes in is that of the prophecies: the basins and the cards. He never doubts the vision of his death he sees in the prophetic waters, lying face down, dressed in denim and with one arm folded under his head as a pillow. Thus he arranges the body of his double, Patricio Aragonés, and thus he is found at the end. Previous to the "error-free waters of the basins" it had been the cards which had arranged the destiny of the nation and anticipated its history. His mother, too, had consulted a circus fortune-teller who noticed that the newborn baby had no lines on his hand, a sure sign he would be king.

The "prophecies" towards the end of the book tend to be either self-fulfilling or simply predictions carried out by the predictor, while a manipulation of time and space adds to the circularity of motion in the novel. If the crew of torturers working for Saenz de la Barra anticipate conspiracies "long before they started incubating in people's thoughts" (215), it is because their actions provoke the rebellions that must be suppressed. The general's frustration mounts with his helplessness toward the end of his life, accentuated by the notion that he can't give an order before it is carried out. The general, fed up finally with Saenz de la Barra, "foresees" that he will be found hanging from a lamp post by his feet with his genitals stuck in his mouth, the streets to the embassies having been cordoned off to prevent him from seeking asylum.

The tightly knit structure of the novel reinforces the circularity of the action. Each section begins with the finding of the body in the decrepit palace and flashes back to explain episodes from the incredibly long life of the dictator. Thus on the second page we see juxtaposed such incidents from the end as the rosebushes covered with lunar dust, which are described as having been a place for lepers during an earlier period, "the great days of the house" (8). Even before those days the patriarch's daily routine would include deciding the destiny of the nation, not by himself but with the commandant of the forces of occupation. He resolves household matters with the same simplicity with which he orders that the clock strike twelve twice to make life seem longer, just as daylight saving time seems to lengthen the days. The general always seems old, though we see him at different periods of his life; the passage of time with respect to him is indicated, as in the title, by the word *autumn*. Thus we see him early in his autumn, at its fullness, or in its last frozen leaves, but never earlier than his autumn. Often seen as childish, as when he gives toys to his mother or to Manuela, and often described as a child, he is always presented within the framework of senility: a second childhood.

In his historical references García Márquez also destabilizes our conceptions of time. Sir Walter Raleigh is associated with prehistoric tortoises, and sloops are clustered around the old slave port, "the former slave platform still in use" (170). In a scene of masterful juxtaposition of time and space that challenges our sense of history by giving us alternatives to the official story, we see the American marines in the foregound of the port and the three caravels of Columbus approaching in the background, as the narrative shifts from the general to an aborigine reacting to the arrival of the Spaniards. Instead of hearing once again the point of view of Columbus, who depicted the Indians as cowardly, childish, and scandalously nude, we hear the other side of the story: strangers arriving who talk funny, "decked out like the jack of clubs in all that heat," while the Indians were "as normal as the day our mothers bore us" (44). But the narrators here are at once aborigines and current inhabitants of the Caribbean observing the Europeans, as the imitation of the antiquated language makes clear, for example, when the Spaniards shout to each other "how well-formed, of beauteous body and fine face" (43) the Indians are. In the closing of the circle, when the body is finally accepted as the general's and his death can be believed at last, it can be announced to the world that "the uncountable time of eternity had come to an end" (251).

Time is so fluid in the novel that it seems paradoxically static at times; from the first relation of the discovery of the body, when the birds' wings stir time, up to the final acceptance of the corpse's identity, only twenty-four hours have passed, but at the same time a seeming eternity has been recounted. The circular structure of the novel and cyclical concept of time are reinforced by a pattern of relation, evocation, and repetition of key events. The marines and Columbus coincide at the end of the first section; the marines pack up their hospitals and lawns and go home in the second; the patriarch remembers his reasons for allowing them to occupy in the third.

In the final section the ambassador suggests the excuse of an outbreak of yellow fever for an occupation, which is certainly a recurrence of other, earlier colonizations. At the same time the taking away of the sea in numbered pieces to Arizona is related, an incident that has been referred to in various passages along the way.

Two parallel techniques are introduced by García Márquez in this novel which work together to constantly shift the focus of the narration and challenge assumptions: the length of the sentences, including an original use of punctuation, and the multiple narrators, with incorporation of different kinds of language within a single sentence. The opening sentence of the first section is of normal length, and thereafter relatively short sentences begin each section and are used to refer to the main focus of the narration: the finding of the body. The sentences get progressively longer within the sections, and finally the last section is made up of a single sentence. Within every sentence the point of view constantly shifts. The plural narrator, representing those who discover the body, and presumably the people, moves gradually to an omniscient narrator recounting the events in the patriarch's life and the occupation by the marines. The plural narrators, who have never actually seen him, cannot relate these events directly because they are too young. Incorporated within the recounting of events by the outside narrator are exclamations of various protagonists within the story, including the general himself. The voices directed to the general are identified by the tag "general sir," as when the free-lance impostor Patricio Aragonés is found and brought to the palace to become an official impostor. Commands are given by these voices

61

to others, still within the sentence: "silence, the general is screwing" (14). Songs are incorporated as well, and even a telegram: "with the personal order to watch him but to maintain his physical integrity repeat maintain physical integrity . . . signed I, and he repeated, I myself" (141). The expulsion of church people and expropriation of their goods rates a heavy dose of legalese:

> all persons native and foreign who had anything to do with the business of God in any condition and under any title within the borders of the country and up to fifty nautical leagues in territorial waters, and ordered . . . the expropriation of all goods of the church, its houses of worship, its convents, its schools, its arable lands with tools and animals thereon (149).

The harshness of the language is, of course, totally undermined when Leticia Nazareno has them brought back and generously compensated shortly thereafter. The author himself has explained that the use of multiple monologues permits the intervention of numerous unidentified voices, "como sucede en realidad con la Historia y con esas conspiraciones masivas del caribe que están llenas de infinitos secretos a voces" (as really happens in History and with those massive conspiracies of the Caribbean, full of infinite secrets yelled out loud).[3]

The rhythmic flow of the sentences, happily rendered in Gregory Rabassa's translation, substantiates the author's claim that the book is a poem, and that it is musical. Perhaps to offset the shifting point of view, the repetition of certain phrases and parallel constructions create a cadence in the narration and set up patterns identifying the narrators. Particularly obvious is the repetition of the verb *to see* in its various forms: the plural narrators of the beginning section introduce a series of phantasmagoric scenes with the simple phrase "we saw." But their visual testimony is undermined by two things: they had not seen the dictator alive, and they knew of a previous false death. A certain helplessness underlies the repetition of "she watched," referring to Bendición Alvarado's disgust at the evil-living reprobates in the palace, fighting over posts of high command, and similarly the patriarch's weakness vis-à-vis Manuela Sánchez is reiterated by a long series of visions beginning with "he saw." At the beginning of the fourth section, exactly halfway through the book, the plural narrators give us other, similar but different, scenes from the decaying palace, all introduced by the words "we saw," this time undermined by the nervous joke about whether the president, whose corpse they can see, is really dead, and if so, who is going to tell him.

The music of Anton Bruckner, whose work epitomizes the full-fledged Romantic tradition, is associated with the heavy cadences describing the brutal dandy Saenz de la Barra. In fact, García Márquez claims that he constantly listened to Béla Bartók and Caribbean folk music as he was writing the novel. What seems an unlikely combination has its logic when we remember Bartók's love for Hungarian folk music and his efforts to incorporate its rhythms into his compositions. He was making a conscious effort to preserve this tradition, as García Márquez wishes to do with a rewriting of nonofficial versions of history. Thus, Béla Bartók is to Hungarian music what García Márquez is to Latin American fiction; a move toward authenticity and away from excessive outside influences.

63

A discussion of lyricism leads to an examination of the use of imagery, and indeed the images are particularly rich in this work. We have seen the association of autumn with the aging patriarch; two other images stand out among many: his hands, strikingly delicate, and mirrors and their reflections.

García Márquez took a long trip to several Eastern-block countries in the 1950s and wrote a series of articles describing his reactions to these visits. One vision that struck him deeply was that of Stalin's body, laid out in state, with the incongruous hands of a young girl. The vision is repeated often in the novel, beginning with the first description of the dictator's body with the "smooth maiden hands with the ring of power" (11). Always closely associated with power, the hands are nonetheless seldom seen in activity; he shakes a miserly hand and exhibits the hand of someone who would seem to have more compassion, or to belong to a younger person. The rebuff of a woman causes him to place it on his chest, evoking Napoleon's famous posture. For the cripples, lepers, and blind people who inhabit the palace ground, it is a Christlike healing hand: "he touched one of us on the place of our defects with a smooth and wise hand that was the hand of truth, and the instant he touched us we recovered the health of our bodies and the repose of our souls" (232). Like the finely dressed barbarian Saenz de la Barra, the general is at once associated with all kinds of atrocities and somehow removed from them.

In a technique that parallels his undercutting of history by offering multiple voices telling the story, García Márquez uses images in mirrors, glass, the sea, and the lighthouse beacon to create various images of persons and events. Manuela Sánchez, the beauty queen from the dogfight district, appears to the general cloaked in these Borgesian terms: "he saw her appear at the rear door like the image of a dream reflected in the mirror of another dream" (73), terms that put her very existence in doubt. The mirrors of the palace seem a dubious imitation of Versailles as the general sees himself pass by them on his way to bed with fourteen lights. As the novel progresses, these mirrors and their reflections become darkened. The hurricane causes barnacles to grow on them. In calm Decembers the sea itself becomes a glass in which to reflect the city, and is later taken away by the gringos, reflections and all. The former dictators of other countries to whom the general granted asylum are themselves mirrors into his future; after he fleeces them at dominoes, he looks "at himself in the instructive mirrors of their misery" (22). He comes to detest them as much as he detests his own "image in the mirror of misfortune" (43). His identity crisis toward the end is seen as his reflection in the mirror, reversed. A veritable explosion of reflections occurs when other objects with similar properties—chopped ice and rock salt—are seen against the mirrors of the palace. There are vocal reflections, too, when popular, insulting epithets of the people are echoed by parrots until the security forces eliminate the birds as subversive.

If the waters of the basins are the most prophetic, surely the most visually striking images are those seen in the flashing light from the lighthouse, flooding the house "every thirty seconds with green amidst the vapor" (24), even continuing after the selling of the sea makes it preposterous, always a reminder of what is missing. The most literal reflection of the general himself is not seen in mirrors, but in Patricio Aragonés. Having flattened the feet and herniated a testicle of the unfortunate double to make the similarity complete, the illiterate general makes him drink turpentine to forget how to read and write, and only the lack of an authoritative voice keeps him from being an exact replica. The general clings to his double "as if he were himself" (24) in an early hint of doubts of identity, and gives him the same food to eat so if they are poisoned they will die together. Dying from a poisoned dart intended for the general and attended by the general himself, the double becomes, like a talking mirror, the only person to tell the general the truth, repeatedly and without the least respect, in parody of the adulators the general is usually surrounded with. The voice shifts within the same sentence from the double to the general, who is bothered only by Aragonés's lack of gratitude for being set up like a king. In a final reflection of the general's unreal life he sees that he was "condemned not to know life except in reverse, condemned to decipher the seams and straighten the threads of the woof and the warp of the tapestry of illusions of reality without suspecting even too late that the only livable life was one of show, the one we saw from this side which wasn't his, general sir" (250), for the poor, whose voice is represented finally, even in their misery have at least known love, whereas he was only an uncertain vision, "a comic tyrant who never knew where the reverse side was" (251).

García Márquez's poetic background can be seen in many passages of *The Autumn of the Patriarch*, but the clearest imprint and the only direct mention is that of

the Nicaraguan poet Rubén Darío. In addition to the author's obvious admiration for Darío, the choice may also reflect the poet's influence on European, particularly Spanish, poetry. In a reversal of the previous flow of literary movements from the old continent to the new, Darío's modernist movement was the first to go in the other direction. During his stay in Spain, Darío came to know the poets who would later give life to the movement toward aesthetic values and away from philosophical concerns in their poetry, particularly Juan Ramón Jiménez and Vicente Aleixandre, both eventual winners of the Nobel Prize for Literature.

Traces of other literature are bound to be abundant and rich in a well-read author, and in fact *The Autumn of the Patriarch* belongs among a kind of subgenre of Latin American dictator novels which includes works by Ramón del Valle Inclán, Miguel Angel Asturias, Augusto Roa Bastos, and Alejo Carpentier. However, in the case of this novel, the most interesting previous literature to show itself in episodes, characters, and themes is by García Márquez himself. Repetitive in a most original way, he offers us new facets of jewels we have been before. He himself points to what *The Autumn of the Patriarch* shares with *Leaf Storm*: "puntos de vista alrededor de un muerto" (points of view revolving around a dead man).[4] But where the monologues are strictly systematic in the earlier novella, they become richly multiple in the later work. Both Manuela Sánchez of the dogfight district who disappears without a trace into the Caribbean and Leticia Nazareno who is kidnapped and brought back from Jamaica recall Eréndira's endless traipsing and final disappearance in the same thick atmosphere. The mothering both women display toward the patriarch emphasizes his childishness, relationships not unlike that of Senator Onésimo Sánchez and Laura Farina in the short story "Death Constant Beyond Love." But the most interesting points of contact by far can be made between this novel and its immediate predecessor, *One Hundred Years of Solitude*. If García Márquez had written about a dictator in a straight biographical fashion, as he once thought of doing, the protagonist might have resembled the Colonel; as the story is told, the dictator is a composite of many dictators and reflects aspects of some of the José Arcadios and Aurelianos of the earlier novel. But more than characters, situations and attitudes are repeated, often in a grotesque parody of what had gone before. If José Arcadio drives Ursula mad with his manner of proving things, such as the existence of God by daguerreotype prints, the search for proof that the general is indeed himself and dead when the plural narrators have his corpse in front of them is absurd on a similar level. The toys that Pietro Crespi introduces into the Buendía household become the gifts of a senile child to the patriarch's mother and desired women. The polyps and microscopic crustaceans in the general's armpits reflect the unnamed scourge in the same area of the Colonel's afflicted body when he returned from the wars, themselves much like the federalist wars that gave rise to the patriarch's power in the first place. The banana company's intervention becomes a military presence down to the dismantling of the sea; the abandoned state of the areas after the outsiders leave is similar, as is their separation from the locals during the occupations. The beauty queen of the dogfight district is a caricature of Fernanda, though the roles are somewhat reversed; Manuela manages to disappear, ridiculing the power of the general, who creates an eclipse for her but is unable to find her, whereas Fernanda, so desperately sought by Aureliano Segundo, is surely the most ridiculous figure in Macondo, with her nightgown with a small, lace-framed hole in it, her imaginary diseases and doctors, and her son who would be pope. Bendición Alvarado's "miraculously" painted sheet, which bears her likeness just as St. Veronica's veil bore Christ's, reflects the "miracle" of Remedios the Beauty's virginal assumption into heaven amidst Fernanda's precious Brabant sheets.

Bendición Alvarado shares several characteristics with Ursula, though neither can be called a matriarch in the sense that the general is a patriarch. Both are hardworking, practical women, without the sense of history, grandiose rather than visionary, of some of the patriarchal figures. Ursula repeatedly tries to ward off ruin and decay, as does Amaranta Ursula years later, by scrubbing and cleaning; Bendición finds in horror that no matter how much she scrubs, the blood cannot be removed from the palace walls by any means. Bendición's frustrations at the silly gringo gewgaws are as useless as Ursula's exasperations at the mad experiments and gypsy acquisitions of José Arcadio. Bendición becomes a grotesque object of veneration and capitalism after her death, as people grab at her corpse for relics to sell, while Ursula, in her extreme old age, becomes a doll for little Amaranta Ursula and Aureliano to play with.

The innocent Remedios Moscote, married prematurely to the Colonel, has her perverted reflection in the schoolgirls, substituted by waterfront whores, that so fascinate the aged general; the irritation like a rock in the Colonel's shoe is much more painful and appropriately placed in the general, caused by longing for Manuela Sánchez. Petra Cotes's association with the proliferation of animals and thus with Aureliano Segundo's wealth gives her comfort and leverage if not power; the patriarch's ability to make trees bear fruit and animals grow by pointing may seem an absurd exaggeration, but certainly his pointing to people to make them prosper in the same phrase is a fine-tuned metaphor for the corruption inevitably surrounding such a figure. The unnamed examiner of the destiny of others, including the patriarch, who reads cards and palms brings Pilar Ternera to mind, while the general's early activities, bringing back stray husbands with ropes around their necks, reflects the arrival of Amaranta Ursula in Macondo leading Gaston with a silk leash. Rebeca reverts to her primitive behavior of eating dirt when tensions rise; the sick people eat the salt of the earth as well, but only as passed out to them by the miraculous hand of the patriarch. If in the Buendía household the last Aureliano is the only person to have been engendered in love, the palace of the patriarch rates even worse: it is a place where no happy person had ever slept. In nature, too, wind is a common denominator for these two novels and is also the cause of Eréndira's misfortune; the patriarchal city survives the hurricane "so terrible that it did not deserve its woman's name" (90) and even gives the patriarch new wealth as he sells the aid poured in from around the world. The flaming tallow balls that announce evil are skirted by the patriarch, as are so many earthly disorders and ominous eclipses, but the orange disks that cross the Macondo sky are harbingers of death. The Hindus of the Caribbean nation fulfill the functions of the gypsies of Macondo as well as the vendors on the Street of the Turks. And finally the sad bits of paper with which the ancient patriarch tries to jog his memory are like the useless labels made in Macondo during the insomnia plague.

It is difficult to imagine a more political novel than *The Autumn of the Patriarch*, reflecting as it does the concerns of its author. In preparation for this novel, seventeen years in the making, García Márquez read numerous biographies of dictators and went to live in Spain under the dictatorship of Francisco Franco for more firsthand experience of day-to-day living under a tyrant. He intended the book to be a composite, though he admits he was so immersed in the presence of Juan Vicente Gómez of Venezuela that the book probably has more of his traits than those of the many others. Gómez, for example, used to have his death announced to see the reactions of those around him. He died peacefully in his bed after having governed with an iron hand for nearly thirty years. In his readings García Márquez also found that "Papa Doc" Duvalier, while dictator of Haiti, once decreed that all black dogs of his realm be killed, because he was convinced that one of his enemies had turned himself into a black dog to escape vengeance. Dr. José Gaspar Rodríguez Francia of Paraguay ordered all men over twenty-one to marry, and Maximiliano Hernández Martínez of El Salvador had all the public utility wiring covered with red paper to fight a measles epidemic; he also invented a magic pendulum to swing over his food to tell whether it had been poisoned. More recently, the discovery of the crimes of African emperor Jean-Bedel Bokassa, including canibalism, leave little to exaggeration or imagination. Unfortunately, it is not difficult to find other examples. The list of the patriarch's characteristics common to other dictators would be long indeed, and Omar Torrijos complimented his friend García Márquez by telling him: "Todos somos así como tú dices" (we're all just like you say).[5] But I would like to turn tables on time, as the author so often does, by pointing out just one detail of the novel that predates a similar happening in reality. Saenz de la Barra, the dictator's unimaginably bloodthirsty righthand man whose excesses in brutality are reflected in his immeasurable acquisitiveness, had, when he was finally purged, three thousand pairs of Italian boots. When the Marcos family fled the Philippines for their "golden" exile in Hawaii in 1986, Imelda's closet was filled with three thousand pairs of shoes, most unused. And to look ahead, if the Latin American nations have not yet had to sell their territorial waters to pay off foreign bankers, it's difficult to imagine what else they have that could come close to the astronomical figures they now owe.

NOTES

1. In a superb study of *One Hundred Years of Solitude*, with mention of García Márquez's earlier work, Mario Vargas Llosa makes a list of the author's recurring preoccupations, or *demonios*; see his *García Márquez: Historia de un deicidio* (Barcelona: Barral, 1971).

2. *The Autumn of the Patriarch* (New York: Avon, 1976) 32. All quotations are form this edition; page numbers are noted parenthetically.

3. *El olor de la guayaba. Conversación con Plinio Apuleyo Men-*

doza (Barcelona: Bruguera, 1982) 88. This and other quotations, as well as many thoughts and ideas attributed to García Márquez come from this work.

    4. *El olor* 58.
    5. *El olor* 89.

CHAPTER THREE

Love in the Time of Cholera

The love so painfully lacking in *The Autumn of the Patriarch* abounds in *Love in the Time of Cholera* to such an extreme that if the subject had been treated with less depth, the novel might be thought of as bad romantic fiction. On one level the story is framed around an unusual love triangle—husband and wife in a marriage of fifty years and a man who loves the wife for all that time, patiently waiting his turn, which begins after the husband's death.

It is, of course, the number of years and consequently the ages of the protagonists that give García Márquez space to develop the story into a complex multilevel work whose themes go beyond love to a study of aging, sexuality, and death. Constructed on the solid basis of character development and relationships, and reinforced by strikingly visual imagery, the work once again calls into question the reader's concepts of time and reality. At the same time the dosage of social criticism is served with such wit, humor, and grace that it could almost go unnoticed.

García Márquez has said that he is the kindest man in the world, that he has an extreme love for his friends, and that he always has compassion for his characters, no matter how unlovable they might be.[1] He seems to have given free reign to those feelings in this novel. But the romantic notions are grounded in reality; if the lover swears his love will last a lifetime, we must see that whole life, including the infirmities of old age as well as the insecurities of youth. We feel the tensions within the various relationships as well as the moments of hope and delight, and the effects of outside circumstances as well as the most intimate feelings of the lovers.

The love that is so pervasive throughout this long novel is inextricably linked with Florentino Ariza and, through him, with the reading of literature and the writing of letters. Florentino is the personification of the most romantic notions of love; it rules his life. He not only promises to love forever, he does it. His actions and thoughts are always linked in some way to his love for Fermina Daza, and he is absolutely sure that no one on the face of the earth has as great a capacity for love as he does. His existence within the novel, when not directly related to Fermina, still revolves around love, for he loves others and discovers "what he had suffered many times without realizing it: that one can be in love with several people at the same time, and feel the same pain for all of them, without betraying any of them."[2]

Before his inglorious deflowering on the boat trip, he had the intention of keeping himself strictly and technically pure for Fermina. As a result of that incident he discovers that his unrequited but still intact love for her could be substituted by earthly passion. The discovery changes him radically, and from that moment his love-making becomes so prodigious that fifty years later he counts 622 "amores continuados" (ongoing loves) in his little black book, which he calls, simply and discreetly, "Them" (210).

But lest we think of these relationships as mere one-night or one-month stands, the novelist carefully develops several of these minor characters so that we see Florentino's very real affection, and even love, for some of them: Sara Noriega, to whom he dedicates spiritual love from the waist up and physical love from the waist down; the unfortunate Olimpia Zuleta, for whom he plants and tends the rosebushes in the cemetery; the equally unfortunate América Vicuña, who happens to be in love with him at the time when Fermina Daza becomes a widow. Perhaps most interesting among his loves is the unconsummated one, Leona Cassini, actually the woman of his life though he doesn't realize it. While rejecting his sexual advances both in youth and in old age, she tenderly cares for him on a daily basis over the many years he works at the Riverboat Company. Even his uncle wants him to marry Leona, but Florentino must keep himself free for Fermina Daza.

For Florentino, love constitutes his entire reason for being. After Fermina's rejection and his trip he finds himself adrift for a time, suffering from jealousy and depression. But when the couple returns from Europe and he sees Fermina Daza, the vision gives him the certainty that the only way to maintain hope for eventually winning her love is to succeed at work. All the jobs he does at the Riverboat Company, beginning with the most menial and insignificant, are done for Fermina Daza. Indeed, in a way he cannot foresee in the beginning, the job offers him the only place where he can be happy with her: in the luxury cabin of one of his ships.

Like any good romantic soul Florentino constantly links love with suffering, which he seeks and which his mother encourages: " 'Take advantage and suffer all you can, now that you're young,' she would say to him, 'things like this won't last your whole life' " (89). Tránsito is wrong that it won't last a lifetime in his case; she underestimates his capacity for love. The suffering of love is not limited to the psychological kind: Florentino's propensity for a certain constipation/diarrhea syndrome is accentuated by love-related tensions, and perhaps intensified by such ingestions as the bouquet of roses he consumes while reading a letter from Fermina. To his horror and Fermina's perplexity his long-awaited visit to her has to be postponed by intestinal urgencies which make him remember his very first letter to her, on which a most unromantic bird left its untidy mark.

Florentino's love of reading and need to write are intricately related to his role as lover. He begins the courtship with Fermina by reading, and sometimes pretending to read, in the park across the street from the Daza house. What he reads is of great interest: everything. Not selective like Juvenal Urbino, Florentino reads all he can, preferring poetry, especially of love, but not shying away from anything. He devours the series Biblioteca Popular, which includes everything from classical Greek and Latin poets to what snobs would call pulp novels. He had started young, when his mother bought him books by Nordic authors sold as children's stories. He knows what he likes without worrying about what is good, and has a remarkable ability to imitate verses. He rereads his favorites so much that the pages finally disintegrate.

His literary avocation serves him well. Much of his relationship with Fermina Daza is conducted through letters, and when she marries and he cannot continue the correspondence, he writes letters for other, less literary lovers. In fact, he becomes the Cyrano de Bergerac for so many of the town's lovers that he is often named the godfather of children born to couples for whom he had composed messages of love. In some cases he finds himself in a passionate correspondence with himself, for both of a pair of lovers use his services.

The greatest body of his letters had been written during Fermina's long visit to her cousin, when his job at the telegraph office was an invaluable aid in keeping in contact with her. The episode may be based on the early relationship of the author's parents: his mother belonged to an important family in town and was courted by a telegraph operator whom the family considered unworthy. They sent her on a long trip, but were unable to break the contact, for the suitor and his colleagues kept telegrams coming to her throughout her absence. In this real-life case the family gave in, and the marriage took place soon afterward.

Florentino writes as tirelessly as he reads—including many pages his mother talks him out of sending, for she fears Fermina will be overwhelmed. Fermina responds, but her letters are without the floridity of his; in fact, they are filled with details of daily life so that they resemble a ship's log. The correspondence is continued so faithfully and so long that the letters end up sounding as familiar as spousal letters might be.

But if writing letters gives Florentino a role in the town's love life, it also creates problems for him at work. First hired as secretary for his ability to write, he soon realizes, to his uncle's chagrin, that even the most serious business letters come out sounding like love letters. Florentino is unable to delyricize his writing and has to be moved to other departments. He thinks of trying to capitalize on his talent by publishing a manual for lovers, and perhaps some form love letters for others to imitate, but his mother is not persuaded that it would be a worthwhile investment for her savings.

After years of this vicarious writing, he at last finds himself able to write again to Fermina Daza. Always more successful with her on paper than in person, he rebounds from her rejection on the day of her husband's burial and composes a letter that turns out to be just what she wanted and expected. The letters that follow, more circumspect than any he managed to write for the Riverboat Company, become of vital interest to Fermina, and in fact give her reason to keep living. These are mature letters, meditations on life, love, old age, and death. They can be thought of as constituting the novel itself in different form, just as Melquíades's parchments tell the story of *One Hundred Years of Solitude*.

Florentino may have inherited both his greatest capacities—for love and for writing—from his father. He always kept the notebook his father left behind, and he is astonished by two characteristics of the notebook: the handwriting is identical to his, though he chose his from a manual, and his father's attitude toward love. He finds a sentence written by his father, many years before his birth, which he thought was his: "The only thing that hurts about dying is that it isn't for love" (233). Florentino's mother, much more practical than romantic, nevertheless must have been very affectionate; indeed,

Tránsito Ariza sometimes looks at her son with more concupiscence than maternal affection, and she consoles him with "recursos de novia" (a girlfriend's resources) when Fermina rejects him (189). But it is one of the 622 occasional lovers who best describes Florentino's capacity as a lover and explains the reasons: "because there couldn't be anyone on earth as needy for love" (391). Hildebranda had seen him slightly differently: old and sad, but all love.

The two other protagonists, Fermina Daza and her husband, love too, but on a more human scale. For although Fermina feels sorry for Florentino after her disillusion at seeing him leads to her implacable decision to break with him, she never once doubts the wisdom of her choice. When Florentino is the subject of conversation among a group of her friends, but no one of them can conjure up a mental image of him, she understands why: Florentino is much too much of a nonentity for her. She understands in maturity that he is not the type of man she would have chosen.

Neither Fermina nor Juvenal Urbino is in love when they marry. The doctor is attracted to her great pride, which pricks his own when she immediately rejects him, and to her strength. In contrast to the opinion of the public Juvenal Urbino is a weak man, as Fermina discovers when they return from their wedding trip and begin to live with his mother. Always the hypocrite, he blames the troubles on the institution of marriage rather than on the stifling atmosphere in the family house.

Until her father announced to her that they were in financial ruin, Fermina received the doctor only with rebuffs. While her pride is partly responsible for this attitude, she really does not seem interested in the doctor. Something of a shady character, whose suspicious business with mules turns out to be his only legitimate one, Lorenzo Daza immediately begins a kind of courtship of Urbino as soon as he sees there is an interest. Everyone in town considers the doctor to be the best catch among the eligible bachelors, but still Fermina resists. Then she receives anonymous letters threatening her life if she continues her "relationship" with the doctor, and given her contrary character, it is possible that these letters have the opposite of the desired effect. In any case, her father's laconic description of their financial state makes her realize she is on her own, and she soon permits Urbino to visit.

They do come to love each other during their long stay in Europe. Juvenal Urbino is a well-instructed man, and he understands that Fermina's pride is often a cover-up for fear. He is especially delicate in their first lovemaking, for he realizes that she is terrified. His patience pays off, and a real tenderness develops and continues to grow, except for their two periods of greatest difficulty, throughout their lives. Each expresses this love late in life in their own way. The somewhat unverbal doctor waits an instant after he should be dead to give Fermina time to arrive, so he can say to her, "Only God knows how much I loved you" (64). A few months later, in one of her feverish efforts to get rid of things, she says of his belongings, "People a person loves should die with all their belongings" (75), a pronouncement bordering on reproach, so characteristic of her mania of blaming others for everything.

Nevertheless, neither ever equals the extremes of

Florentino in questions of love. Fermina learns when her father proposes another suitor that one can live not only without love, but even against it. At the time she still believes she is in love with Florentino, and has no doubt that she could never love the other; but she also has come to an awareness that there might be some exaggeration in Florentino's attitude, and that maybe she is capable of living without him after all. Her disenchantment has already begun, and it is not only with the person of Florentino but also with the idea of love itself. As for Dr. Urbino, he is much too scientific, rational, and calculatingly cold to approach the pure romanticism of his rival. When he marries below his social class, he marries for practical reasons. His choice reflects what he thinks is important: Fermina's good looks, charm, intelligence, and pride will allow her to deal with her new social ambience, to play a proper role as the doctor's wife, and to take care of him as well as to perform all the wifely tasks that await her. She is useful adornment, as befits the wife of a man like Urbino.

Class differences play an important part in this novel, and are often embodied in the contrasts among the protagonists. For whereas the doctor keeps up with European literature, especially French—except that he refuses to read Zola—he is not the least bit interested in the literature of his own country, or indeed of any New World country. Moreover, there is no sense in which he reads for pleasure; he reads what he is supposed to read, because he is supposed to read it. The contrast with Florentino is acute, and is repeated in music. The doctor's standard question when he wants to begin a friendly conversation is about musical preferences; when he asks

Florentino, who has had no music appreciation course but has a genuine love for music, the reply is not satisfactory to Urbino. His scornful reaction is: "I see. . . . It's in style" (261).

García Márquez enjoys making fun of the upper classes of Latin America, especially in their servile and absurd imitation of Europeans and scorn for their own cultures. Urbino's compatriots are more or less satisfied if their chauffeurs have a clean shirt, but Urbino, who studied in Europe, insists that his coachman wear the livery uniform and top hat—not only anachronistic but downright cruel in the climate of the Caribbean. Others in his class, those with long names, are also implacable with themselves—the women, for example, wearing fur coats in that tropical climate. Some of the episodes seem drawn out of the sixteenth-century novel *Lazarillo de Tormes*, one of whose employers is so poor he has nothing to eat but is too noble to work. His "honor" forces him to go outside after mealtime with a toothpick to fool others. He is the poorest of Lazarillo's owners, and in a fine irony Lazarillo ends up begging to support him. The women in the Caribbean who hock their jewelry to Tránsito Ariza and then rent it back to go to parties are victims of the same hypocritical malady. It is an irony fully appreciated by Florentino's uncle, León XII. Accused of being rich, the self-made owner of the Riverboat Company replies: "Not rich. . . . I'm a poor man with money. It's not the same" (229). Fermina Daza recognizes late in life that her husband's attitude, covered as always with hypocrisy, accounts for the fact that they, like so many of their social counterparts, had been to Europe several times but knew nothing of their own country.

Fermina Daza, in more ways than the obvious, forms a bridge between the doctor, representing the upper class, and Florentino, whose status as bastard underscores his low origins. Her own status is rather nebulous; she is not from the town, and her father appears to have money, but he seems at once low class and shady. He sends Fermina to the best school, which also represents the state of the upper class: for need of cash it is now forced to take students other than children with long last names. The school keeps its pretensions in spite of financial difficulties, not unlike the ladies who rent back their hocked jewelry from Tránsito Ariza, thus enriching a member of the lower classes. While Fermina learns all the social graces at the school, she never accepts the hypocrisy shared by the other students. It is indeed perhaps her lower status that solidifies her characteristic pride, so closely linked with fear or inferiority. Fermina shares a certain populist attitude with her daughter-in-law, much more like herself than either of her children. Finally it is her daughter's haughty uptight morality that causes Fermina to banish her from her house forever; Ofelia's verbalization of what others think of Fermina's relationship with Florentino actually pushes Fermina to accept Florentino's advances in their twilight years.

Fermina is not immune to consumerism, but her purchases in Europe indicate her down-to-earth taste. Instead of the famous-label Ferry shoes she "should" buy, she prefers the Italian shoes with no label; her collection of fans is not decorative but practical; she succumbs and buys fancy perfume, but wears it only once because it confuses her sense of her own identity. She also acquires a cosmetic set that is all the rage, but in an act of defiance, for she takes it to parties with her when the act of powdering oneself in public is considered indecent.

In fact, as she gets older, Fermina's sense of herself becomes stronger. If she had fallen into the temptation to overbuy, she finally recuperates her need for space and begins to get rid of things. But her impulse to free more space conflicts with her frugality, and she is unable to burn things; she finally opts for putting them where they can't be seen. The riverboat trip toward the end of her life takes on special significance in this context. She takes a dozen cotton dresses, her toiletry, a pair of shoes for getting off and on the boat, her house slippers for the time on the boat, and nothing else: "the dream of her life" (433).

This new sense of herself occurs after the death of Juvenal Urbino, and there are several other manifestations of it. She had been aware for years that she was living in her husband's world, and that her role was that of a high-class servant, but resisted giving too much thought to something that would undoubtedly make her unhappy. Alone now in her widowhood, she tries to recover the vestiges of her identity, while, ironically, the townspeople, who had always used her own name to refer to her, begin to call her "la viuda de Urbino" (Urbino's widow; 412). At the same time she misses her husband and wanders around the solitary house, in which she feels a guest, wondering who is more dead: the deceased or the survivor.

In spite of this borrowed life, during the two periods of marital difficulties it was the doctor who finally gave in, for Fermina Daza is not only strong and proud but stubborn. In the episode of whether there was soap in the bathroom, her refusal to give in even though she knows she is wrong may be seen as an early rebellion against the role of servant she is made to play. Urbino finally yields because he wants to get back in his bed. The second episode is more complex. Aside from the jealousy, pain, and feelings of betrayal, Fermina is also reacting out of pride. She is most upset that the woman with whom Juvenal is having the affair is black, and furious that he told the priest, making public her shame. Having left the home, her self-esteem will not allow her to return, and once again, after two years, Urbino gives in. Her delight at seeing him does not alter her plan to get even through silence: it is a punishment he has earned.

The importance of her new status as widow is that now she can love Urbino in her own way, for she is certain that he is present, "still alive, but without his male caprices or his patriarchal demands, without the draining necessity for her to love him with the same ritual of inopportune kisses and tender words with which he loved her" (409). Fermina is only one of several women in the novel whose first taste of freedom occurs at widowhood, not unlike Molière's *Les femmes savantes*. The social criticism of the economic dependence of women is underscored by contrasting episodes concerning women's fates; perhaps Fermina marries for money, as one of Florentino's lovers accuses her, but it is clear that her choices are extremely limited. Her aunt Escolástica is not so lucky. Her advice to the young Fermina is to accept the suitor, for if not, she'll end up like herself—dependent on the charity of a whimsical brother. Escolástica pays the price for trying to help her niece escape her harsh fate.

After having raised the girl, she is thrown summarily out of the house, and no one hears more from or about her until news of her death is received thirty years later.

But the internal pressure to marry is as strong as necessity, and finally convinces Fermina to accept Urbino's proposals. Not convinced by his beauty, wealth, or glory, she gives in, "rattled by fear of the opportunity she was losing and the imminence of her twenty-first birthday, which was her personal limit for giving herself over to her destiny" (282). Indeed, her education has been for this: she studied at the high school, "where the young ladies of society had been learning for two centuries the art and profession of being diligent and submissive wives" (80). The oppression of women, then, crosses class lines in that the major difference between Fermina's life and that of poor women is that she has other servants to help her in her role as servant, and she has to give in to the sexual demands of one man instead of many. Age treats women differently, too. For women there are only two ages: the marriageable age, up to twenty-two, and the age of being old maids. Those who marry don't count their age in relation to years lived, but to how many years are left before they die.

Perhaps Florentino Ariza's observations about old age and death in his autumnal letters to Fermina included these thoughts about aging in men and women. For he had spent many hours in the park observing the old couples taking their walks, learning that the process is indeed discriminatory. In middle age the men seem to grow more dignified, while the women just kind of fade; but in old age it is the men who become helpless, while the women must guide them across the street, avoiding

87

puddles and corpses of beggars, and up and down steps, at the same time dancing through the mine field of masculine pride. For this reason Florentino fears death less than age, for he knows that when he arrives at that helpless point, he will finally have to give up hope of winning the love of Fermina Daza.

Next to love the aging process is the book's most important theme, and the two are linked in a defiance of society's prejudice against the sexuality of old people.[3] García Márquez keenly observes the process itself and continually mentions details of its encroachment; at the same time he proclaims a dignified old age and the right to companionship and pleasure. Fermina Daza's two children are typical of society's cruel and thoughtless attitude in this respect. We have seen how Fermina banished her daughter Ofelia from her house forever, "for being insolent and evil-thinking" (440). While her son is not against Fermina's relationship with Florentino, and even encourages it, we see his shallow thinking in a conversation with Florentino. The young doctor believes that old people should be segregated and sent to asylums, ostensibly to keep each other company. His reasoning is that it must make them sad to be around young people. Of course it never occurs to him to ask them, or offer them a choice.

For Juvenal Urbino the worst of growing old is the sensation that he is losing his sense of justice; on the other hand, he is consoled by his lack of sexual desire. To Tránsito Ariza the loss of memory is so crippling that it makes her unable to continue her business; she can't remember how to deal with her accounts, and in fact she has trouble remembering who she is. León XII is most concerned with people feeling sorry for him, and it is for this reason that he gives up the business and refuses even to be consulted about matters of the Riverboat Company. Nostalgia becomes more intense for everyone. But it is the great lover Florentino Ariza who sees the brightest side. For all his worry about baldness, his fall, and other infirmities, he is the one who sees that love can be even more intense with age, for it is the last chance.

In typical García Márquez fashion, there is a circular pattern to aging, and he observes on many occasions the return to characteristics of infancy and the change in role of parents and children. Leona refuses Florentino's advances late in life because it would be like making love to her son. The widows remember all their lives how they raised their husbands until the last day, feeding them and changing their diapers and playing with them to dissipate their terror of going out into the street to see reality. América Vicuña has the sensation that she is sixty years older than Florentino, instead of the other way around, when he begins to give her excuses for his lack of attention. Leona Cassini cares for him at her birthday party as if he were an old baby, wiping up the food he spills and putting a bib on him. Fermina, on that final boat trip, rejects the camellias he sends, not only because they evoke the past, but also because they seem so childish to her.

Just as he is the most intense at love, Florentino is the most philosophical about age. When Prudencia Pitre comments that Juvenal Urbino's accidental death while chasing a parrot was absurd, Florentino replies that death has no sense of the ridiculous, "especially at our age" (391). It is also Florentino who sees death not as a horizontal torrent, but as a bottomless pit where memory trickles away. Florentino is a patient man, and the delicacy with which he seduces Fermina in the luxury cabin of his boat is a work of art; their companionship during the last stage of their long lives is a delicious defiance of shallow stereotypes.

This attitude stands in glaring contrast with the early episode of the suicide of Jeremiah de Saint-Amour when he reached his sixtieth birthday. Aided by his dignified secret lover he takes cyanide, feeds it to his dog, and wills his belongings to her. Juvenal Urbino is shocked that she hadn't turned him in, but her reply is that she loved him too much for that. Fermina understands her attitude better than the righteous doctor, for she knows more about love. Saint-Amour's death is not seen as undignified or reprehensible; rather, as a pity, for in a Proustian way evoked by his name he deals with time by looking back, and cannot envision anything positive in the future. As Juvenal says to his dead friend; "Asshole. . . . The worst was already over" (11). This waste is heightened by a vision of what could have been. Indeed it is hard to imagine the suffering of old age, as we see it in the other characters, as being worse than the agony of Jeremiah de Saint-Amour during the year preceding his suicide.

As usual, García Márquez plays with our established concepts of time. As the title suggests, he often connects it with some event, such as the cholera epidemic or the civil war, but those events are too repetitive to fix a concrete time. The novel is replete with foreshadowings, premonitions, and prophecies, including one that León XII doesn't realize he is making. Reprimanding Florentino for the lyricism of his business letters, he rejects his nephew's excuse that he is only interested in love. "The bad thing is," his uncle told him, "that without river navigation, there's no love" (231). It is the same Uncle León XII whose only regret in life is that he won't be able to sing at his own funeral. After Juvenal Urbino's death and the presence of his ghost begins to fade, Florentino Ariza reappears in Fermina's life like a "fantasma atravesado" (an oblique ghost; 384).

The author of *Love in the Time of Cholera* also contin- ues his tradition of making more flexible the lines sepa- rating reality from appearances. The point is sometimes to uncover hypocrisy, as when the social press praises in glowing terms an opera no one could see because of the smoke from the lamps, or when Juvenal Urbino's real likeness at death is unacceptable because he is wearing an expression of fear. The worst period of the Daza/ Urbino household is seen in the town as their best, and Sister Franca de la Luz offers to erase the cause of Fermina's expulsion from the school's records if she will agree to see Juvenal Urbino. Most interesting are two brief mentions of madness: Florentino dances at carnival with a girl who has escaped from a madhouse because she wanted to dance, and Sara Noriega ends up in a mad- house singing such obscene songs she has to be isolated from the others. In both cases the question of the relativ- ity of madness is pronounced: one wonders who is really crazy. But the most strangely lyrical contrast between reality and appearances is the one that gives title to the novel; in order to be alone together finally, it becomes necessary for Florentino to put up the flag of cholera on the ship of love, so no one will bother them in their new old lives.

There are a few other reflections of previous works by García Márquez: a fleeting reference to the massacre of the banana company strikers, for example, for which cousin Hildebranda's husband repudiates their son for his involvement. Direct references to other literature include a clear accusation against Joseph Conrad as a seller of arms who does business with Lorenzo Daza; the father of Marcel Proust, who teaches Juvenal Urbino in Europe; and the children's literature from Nordic countries which is more brutal and cruel than the literature one would read at any other age. Somewhat less direct is an episode traced from the Spanish classic *El libro de buen amor* (The Book of Good Love), redone in this novel with a much less happy ending. Olimpia Zuleta pays with her life for allowing Florentino to write on her belly, while in the fourteenth-century work the drawing of the lamb grows into a sheep, horns and all, during the husband's long absence. In an image invoking Federico García Lorca's *Los amores de don Perlimplín con Belisa en su jardín* (The Love of Don Perlimplín and Belisa in the Garden) Florentino remembers all his lovers, including "the ones who still rested their heads on the same pillow on which their husbands slept, wearing golden horns under the moon" (368). The granting of a literary prize to a Chinese immigrant and the social consequences form a parody of the prizes themselves: at first no one believes the winner is really the composer of the verses. On the occasion of the death of the Chinese author the poem is reproduced in the paper, but the new generation of poets finds it in such bad taste that now no one doubts the identity of its author. Finally, the attitude toward love on the part of Florentino Ariza makes this novel a better candidate in some ways to be proclaimed "El Amadís de America" than *One Hundred Years of Solitude*, as Mario Vargas Llosa had claimed: no knight of courtly love is more patient than Florentino.[4]

One of the most successful of many images based on reflections is one in which Fermina Daza becomes Alice in Wonderland, returning by way of the mirror. Seated in a restaurant, Florentino catches sight of Fermina, dining with her husband and other friends, leading the conversation "graciously and with a laugh that exploded like fireworks, and her beauty was more radiant beneath the enormous crystal chandelier tears" (313). The tears of Florentino, or the tears of the cut glass of the lamps, reflected in the mirror, frame the image of Fermina. Florentino buys the mirror and continues to see her reflection in it much later, while he reads her letters.

Photographs afford a different kind of reflection, one that freezes an instant and therefore stops the passage of time. Jeremiah de Saint-Amour's photographs of the town's children are saved for the historical archives at the insistence of Dr. Urbino, for these children may never again be as happy as they appear in the photos, and besides the future of the city is in their hands. When Florentino discovers the only two photographs of his father, he sees no resemblance, but later he will discover that a man begins to feel old when he starts to look like his father. In a double time warp Fermina and Hildebranda dress up in the costumes of mid-century ladies to have their picture taken. Looking at themselves in the mirrors beforehand, they laugh at how much they look like the old daguerreotypes of their grandmothers. When they find the copies in old age, the epochs all blend together as an undefined past.

The sea is also a source of reflections, sometimes deceitful. Euclides urges Florentino to descend with him, if only to see the corals, "that other sky beneath the world" (130). Euclides sees all the galleons Florentino wants him to see, but the trinkets he brings to the surface as lost colonial jewels are recognized by Tránsito as worthless baubles. The function of the lighthouse as a refuge for clandestine lovers is paramount, and Florentino does not doubt that sparks of his many loves there reach some sailor at every turn of the light.

Other reflections have no need of mirrors. The two cousins cavort nude as each sees her reflection in the body of the other; repeated years later, this exercise becomes a measure of the passage of time. Fermina also sees her own physical repetition in the person of her young daughter, though the two are so different in character. Dr. Urbino Daza has the same weakness of character his father had, and hasn't the nerve to confront his sister's absurd reproaches to Fermina.

The famous parrot, who becomes infamous as the cause of Urbino's death, had only been allowed into the household because of a verbal slip of the doctor himself. When he banished all animals from the house, he decreed that only those who could speak would be allowed entry. Animal-lover Fermina quickly thinks of getting a parrot, whose verbal virtuosities bring in visitors from all over the Caribbean. The bird learns the European music he hears, imitating Yvette Guilbert in a woman's voice and Aristide Bruant's in a man's, "and ended up with same libertine guffaws that were the masterful mirror of those the servants gave when they heard him sing in French" (33).

Trips, especially on the river, have afforded García Márquez a number of metaphors, so that they almost become microcosms within the story. First Fermina and then Florentino are forced or persuaded to take trips to separate them during their early courtship. In Fermina's case her father insists, and when she returns, the desired effect has taken place and she is no longer interested in Florentino. Tránsito Ariza wants Florentino to go away during the marriage of Fermina and Juvenal, but of course he not only cannot forget, he also refuses to stay away from her presence. In the lovers' final journey, where they meditate on the meanings of life, death, and old age, the trip represents life, and in a way a rerun of the way things could have been. The river also represents the aging process, as it becomes dry, spoiled, and exploited the farther they go upstream.

Two other pervasive presences in the novel must be mentioned: the city and the endless wars. Surely based on Cartagena de Indias, the town shocks Juvenal Urbino when he returns from Europe because of its backwardness, its open sewers, its poor sanitary conditions in general, and its lethargy. Its gossipy society and custom of anonymous letters make it on occasion a protagonist in the story, and its tremendous storms constantly remind us of its location in the New World. Dr. Urbino, frustrated at his unsuccessful efforts to make improvements, sums up sarcastically both its strength and its weakness: " 'How noble this city must be,' he would say, 'when we've been trying for 400 years to destroy it and we haven't succeeded yet' " (155).

Though no principal character is involved in the wars, they are a constant presence and affect the lives of everyone. Florentino is taken for a spy until he convinces his captors that he is just a poor rejected lover. The skirmishes make traveling dangerous at all times, and when Lorenzo Daza is picked up by troops who ask him if he is liberal or conservative, he saves his skin by replying that he is a Spanish subject. Even in the least critical times of the wars there is a curfew. No doubt the wars also account for the number of widows and the military people who drift in and out of town, having fleeting affairs with them. Florentino escapes the draft because he is the only son of an unmarried woman, and he finds himself uselessly writing letters for war veterans who, like the colonel no one writes to, insist on claiming their pensions. Homeless orphans arrive in the city smelling like gunpowder—more uncounted victims of the war. The two plagues of the country, cholera and war, become confused as the officials are ordered to count war victims as plague victims. Urbino sees their bodies floating in the river: "Well, it must be a very strange form of cholera," he said, "because each dead person has his extra shot in the neck" (311).

García Márquez dedicates this novel to his wife, Mercedes, "por supuesto" (of course), for it is a novel of love par excellence. Florentino Ariza can be seen as the embodiment of love, in contrast with the protagonist of *The Autumn of the Patriarch*, who embodies power, and this gives us a clear context for the author's vision of "power as a substitute for love."[5] For Florentino, Fermina Daza is the *diosa coronada* (crowned goddess) mentioned in the epigraph at the beginning of the work; for García Márquez perhaps the goddess is love itself.

NOTES

1. Interview, *Playboy* Feb. 1983.

2. Cited from *El amor en los tiempos del cólera* (Mexico: Diana, 1985) 370, my translation. Other quotations are my translations from this edition.

3. For an excellent study of old age, with considerable attention given to sexuality, see Simone de Beauvoir, *The Coming of Age*, trans. Patrick O'Brien (New York: Putnam, 1972).

4. Mario Vargas Llosa, *García Márquez: Historia de un deicidio* (Barcelona: Barral, 1971).

5. *El olor de la guayaba. Conversación con Plinio Apuleyo Mendoza* (Barcelona: Bruquera, 1982) 115.

CHAPTER 4

The Precursors: Short Novels and Stories

Though any piece of writing done by García Márquez can stand on its own, certain common themes, characters, and situations make it useful to look at some of his short fiction, particularly the earlier stories, in relation to his three long novels and to each other, for García Márquez weaves familiar faces and places in and out of these works. This technique has been seen variously as puzzle pieces, episodes that seem to be seeds of other, more developed episodes, or miniatures. The Eréndira who passes so briefly through the pages on *One Hundred Years of Solitude*, for example, becomes the subject of the film and novella she entitles, complete with heartless grandmother and itinerant photographer. Far from being repetitious, the incidents are as intriguing as life. Just when we thought we knew the judge or the priest from one story, he appears in another, and we see a new aspect of his character which explains something that had gone before, as if people we know superficially one day were to tell us their deepest secrets. Like a detail in a photograph blown up many times, the enlargement shows us what was always there but didn't come to our attention before.

Thus, we meet in *Leaf Storm* the aged widow Rebeca,

while the colonel who attends the ostracized doctor's funeral remembers that other famous colonel, Aureliano Buendía; his daughter Isabel tells us that her father and mother were first cousins. Still another colonel, the one to whom no one writes, also recalls Aureliano and the capitulation known as the Treaty of Neerlandia. Judge Arcadio, such a corrupt tyrant in *One Hundred Years of Solitude*, appears in *In Evil Hour* as more a friend of the bottle than anxious for power.

García Márquez's earliest stories, written when he was barely twenty and under the influence of his favorite writers, especially Woolf, Hemingway, and Faulkner, were published first in periodicals and finally gathered together under the title *Ojos de perro azul* (Eyes of a Blue Dog), the name of one of the stories. The title is characteristic in its bizarre flavor: the stories, for the most part, are excursions into realities and perceptions, and into irrational, surreal, and sometimes nightmarish states of consciousness. In the least successful stories technique becomes more important than content, as if the author were still a bit too self-conscious. Half the stories are an exploration of death: "The Third Resignation" examines the stages, or phases, of death, with many hints of the circular motion of time so perfected in *One Hundred Years of Solitude*. "The Other Side of Death" uses García Márquez's first set of twins in a grotesque look at death and finding one's identity. "Dialogue with a Mirror" repeats the doubling motif with an image reflected in a mirror which gains its own autonomy. The passage of time is mentioned abruptly in "Eva Is Inside Her Cat," a story in which beauty is seen as Eva's enemy,

99

and in which her only contact with the realm of the senses is the desire to eat an orange. In the title story a man and woman who meet only in their dreams cannot remember those dreams upon waking. Perhaps the most Faulknerian of the tales in its atmosphere is "Nabo, the Black Man Who Made the Angels Wait." Nabo, having been kicked by a horse he was grooming, is locked up in the stable because of his resulting madness. His only possible communication is with the retarded girl he had taught how to use the phonograph. The most straightforward of the stories is probably "The Woman Who Came at Six O'Clock," in which a woman who always comes into the bar at six wants an alibi for what she has just done and convinces the barman to say she came at five-thirty that day.

The stories are replete with surprising images and startling cerebral voyages. Mirrors and reflections, doubling, smells and tastes, and a preoccupation with time and death are characteristic threads in these early experimental tales, threads which are to be picked up and fully developed in other works.

Leaf Storm

His first brief novel, *Leaf Storm*, however, is set in a concrete, physical space: Macondo. After an epigraph from *Antigone* and a prologue with narration in the first-person plural, representing the inhabitants of the town, the narrator begins a shift from one to another of the three main characters: the ever-present colonel, his daughter Isabel, and her son, each recounting the story in the first person.

Like *The Autumn of the Patriarch* in its multitude of voices around a dead man, the story gives us first the child's view of the strange situation. His mother is too distant for him to ask her what's going on; it's the first time he has seen a corpse, and his eyes are drawn, even when he wants to look away, to the face that doesn't look like someone who was sleeping, as he had imagined, but like someone who is still alive. When the mother's version takes over, we learn more about the circumstances of this solitary doctor, whose body only her father the colonel would bury, against the wishes of the townspeople. She regrets having brought the child, and realizes that she brought him for the same reason her father insisted on her presence; he wanted to fulfill his sacred promise to bury the doctor, but found himself unable to do it alone. The opening reference to Sophocles's *Antigone* underscores by contrast the lack of a solid relationship between the doctor and the colonel, for Antigone was risking her life to bury her brother against the orders of the king.

Isabel's narration introduces us to the Indian woman Meme, who had lived with the doctor and subsequently disappeared from the town. But her view is still partial, and it has to be the patriach/colonel who fills in the blanks, recalling how and when the doctor first came to town, how the colonel had offered him shelter for eight years against his wife's wishes, and had finally made him leave because the Indian maid was pregnant. The doctor had once saved the colonel's life, but it's not entirely clear that this is the reason the colonel insists on burying him; rather it seems a part of his hermetically enclosed system of honor that requires him to defy all the townspeople, even the priest, in this solitary act.

The colonel's honor and dignity, perhaps even his stubbornness, are the only vestiges of authority he has in the town. Retired from the war years before, he has no real role to play; indeed there is tension between himself and the mayor as well as the priest. But the mayor, hampered by cowardice and alcohol, is no match for the self-assured colonel. The townspeople remain an invisible force, and the last scene shows the coffin flooded by the afternoon light when the Guajiro Indians working for the colonel open the door to take the casket to its resting place.

Little by little the narrators help us fill in the missing parts of the various stories. The first version of the doctor's isolation from the others is that he refused to treat wounded people after one of the many battles of an endless war. But then we find out that he had lost his practice to the banana company doctors well before that. His patients had stopped coming, and finally the other doctors had even questioned his credentials to practice. When he finally says, at the crucial moment of emergency, that he has forgotten all that, to take the patients elsewhere, it has in fact been years since he practiced. The episode has its foreshadowing while the doctor still lives with the colonel. He refuses the entreaties of the colonel's wife to treat the sick maid, Meme. But as he explains to the colonel, Meme is not ill but pregnant, and a little rubbing alcohol will ease her discomfort. There is no need for treatment.

The colonel's honor, or stubbornness, shows up in

other ways. Isabel has married Martín and had a son by him, but after two years Martín disappears with plans for a project, financed by the colonel, and never returns. The colonel suppresses even his own suspicions about Martín: "But I have no right to think he was a swindler because of that. I have no right to think his marriage was only a pretext to convince me of his good faith."[1] Any one else might think so.

The doctor's identity is never revealed. When he cuts himself off from everyone in the town, he also leaves behind the foreign newspapers he used to read, and the colonel realizes he doesn't even know the name of his former guest. But curiously, the doctor is connected in a strange tangent to the town's priest, called the Pup. Both men arrive in Macondo on the same day. For the priest it is a return, since he is from Macondo; for the doctor it almost seems a refuge from something unknown. They oddly resemble each other, not like identical twins, but like brothers. When the people want to burn down the doctor's house with him inside, it is the priest who won't allow it; he bravely protects the only man in the town whom he has never met. This doubling is reinforced by the appearance, in cameo, of the twins of Saint Jerome, and the two sets of twins of Isabel's friend Genoveva García, whose other two children blend into a pattern of repetitions "as if run by some single mechanism; small and upsettingly alike, all six with identical shoes and identical frills on their clothing" (123). In one of the most striking visual images of the novel Isabel looks into the mirror on her wedding day and sees, not her own reflection, but "my mother, alive again, looking at me, stretching her arms out from her frozen space, try-

103

ing to touch the death that was held together by the first pins of my bridal veil" (96).

Reflections across generations are to be seen elsewhere. It is not until Isabel speaks with Genoveva García, who admits she would have stolen Martín away from her, that Isabel realizes with dismay that her son resembles his father.

Leaf Storm contains elements of enough other works by García Márquez to qualify it as a microcosm of the body of his oeuvre. The title itself is made very clear in the prologue, which likens the new inhabitants of the town who appear with the prosperity of the banana company to dead leaves left behind by the swirling wind of some dusty storm—the dregs. They are people with no past and no future; they are impatient and believe only in the present moment. After they abandon Macondo, however, its inhabitants realize the impossibility of rebuilding, for "the leaf storm had brought everything and it had taken everything away" (131).

As in other works of García Márquez, a principal theme in this novella is solitude, here emphasized by the technique of interior monologue. Each narrator is turned inward, and what little dialogue there is is always a quotation within someone else's monologue. The lack of communication between characters is underscored by the silence that reigns in the funereal room and the stifling of any speech among the people present: the boy wants to ask his mother questions, but she seems too distant to him; Isabel reproaches her father, but silently. The colonel's role as patriarch has all the condescension necessary for quelling discussion; his standard reply to any of his wife's criticism is, "You'll understand that too someday" (94).

The heteroglossia formed by the three monologues is successful at maintaining the tensions in the story, and at piquing the reader's curiosity and later filling in the gaps. Some critics find that the boy's speech is too sophisticated for his supposed age. Perhaps he is too philosophical at some points, but his language is quite different from those of the adults, as are his preoccupations. He can't help but wonder what his friends are doing while he is stifling in that room with a corpse, and his thoughts often hint at his incipient sexuality: memories of swimming with his friend Abraham, or of the unfortunate Lucrecia, whom all the boys taunt. Isabel is most concerned with the role of Meme, and the colonel with his honor and power to defy the will of the town. The technique works a bit like a cubist painting in its superposition of planes of reality and interpretation. Like much work by this author, the atmosphere matters more than events in the story.

No One Writes to the Colonel

If *Leaf Storm* focuses on atmosphere, *No One Writes to the Colonel* is a portrait. During the brief period between the two novellas García Márquez had learned how to deal much more effectively with economy of language, and *No One Writes to the Colonel* is not only shorter but much better structured than its predecessor. Many who read it when it first appeared in the periodical *Mito* felt it was the most perfect Colombian novel so far, though critical consideration of it was rather sparse. García Márquez relates a charming anecdote in which he sold the rights to Antioquian publisher Alberto Aguirre at the swimming pool of a Barranquilla hotel instead of calling his wife to have her send him money to cover his expenses.[2]

This colonel is also a picture of dignity with his own special sense of honor, but very different from his counterpart in *Leaf Storm*. For *No One Writes to the Colonel* is about hope rather than power. Hope, and eternal waiting; hope as the only reason to keep going; hope when there is no reason whatever to maintain any; hope against hope.

The colonel has nothing to do but wait. The only structure in his life is his Friday trip to the post office to wait for the mail that never comes. He has been promised a pension for having served in the war, but he has been waiting for many years. At the post office, where he meets and speaks to the doctor without taking his eyes off the mailman, he sheepishly, childishly exclaims that he wasn't expecting anything anyway. Every Friday of his life.

The only other hope in his impoverished life is that his rooster, bequeathed to him by his son who was shot for distributing clandestine literature, will win, entitling him to 20 percent of the bet money even though he doesn't have any money to bet himself. But the colonel and his asthmatic wife don't even have enough money to feed the bird to keep it alive; thus, long before the fight can be scheduled, the cock belongs more to the townspeople, who feed it, than it does to the colonel.

The story opens, again, around a funeral, though the funeral is not in itself the focal point that it is in *Leaf Storm*. Its importance, as the colonel points out to his wife, is that the death is the first one from natural causes in the town for many years. This assertion underscores the pervasive violence in the novella and its atmosphere of political repression; the colonel's son is only one of many victims of the violence. The colonel himself continues in his own quiet way, to pass out clandestine literature, and Don Sabas is the only leader of his party who escaped political persecution and continued to live in town. The very poverty of the town and the lack of anything for the colonel to do are insidious reflections of a constant state of war and persecution, all too real in the Colombia of the period. Even a sign in the tailor's shop, designed to prevent fights, says "Talking Politics Forbidden."

Literature as a theme in the works of García Márquez begins in this novella. In its predecessor there had been an unexplained reference to parchments, which any reader of *One Hundred Years of Solitude* would immediately identify with Melquíades, and to a lampoon nailed to the doctor's door, which brings *In Evil Hour* to mind. But neither reference had any transcendence in the story. In *No One Writes to the Colonel* the issue of literature takes on more importance. First there is the matter of clandestine papers being circulated to inform people of what was not in the day's paper. At the post office with the doctor, the colonel succinctly describes the effects of censorship:

The colonel didn't read the headlines. He made an effort to control his stomach. "Ever since there's been censorship, the newspapers talk only about Europe," he said. "The best thing would be for Europeans to come over here and for us to go to Europe. That way everybody would know what's happening in his own country."[3]

And in a reference to a different type of literature, the colonel refuses to go to town with the clock, which he likens to a showpiece, because if he does, Rafael Escalona will make up a song about him. This popular balladeer follows the ancient tradition of making up songs about events and people in the town—an instance of truly popular oral literature of the kind the medieval troubadours made up from legends and happenings they heard about in their travels.

Censorship is not confined to newspapers, of course. In a new role for an old institution, Father Angel rings twelve bells to announce that the current movie is not fit for anyone to see; the colonel's wife remarks that all the movies in the last year have been pronounced bad for everyone.

It is also in *No One Writes to the Colonel* that we get the first clear-cut role division between women and men in García Márquez. Presented as an aspect of character, the women are concerned about reality, like where the next meal is coming from. The men, here represented by the colonel, are dreamers and quite unconcerned with such matters as relief from starvation. Like the nobleman in the picaresque novel *Lazarillo de Tormes,* who sports a toothpick after mealtime even though he hasn't eaten anything, the colonel is ashamed to try to sell the clock or the picture because people will then know the family is starving. His wife, fed up with high-minded hunger, says she wants food rather than dignity, to which he retorts that even though you can't eat dignity, it sustains you. These dialogues, sprinkled throughout the endless waiting of the narrative, lead to the famous last exchange between the two. To her repeated question, What do we eat?

> It had taken the colonel seventy-five years—the seventy-five years of his life, minute by minute—to reach this moment. He felt pure, explicit, invincible at the moment when he replied:
> "Shit" (83).

The Stories in *Big Mama's Funeral*

Perhaps the most striking image of dignity in García Márquez' work, however, is the figure of a woman. In the story that opens *Big Mama's Funeral,* which is also García Márquez's own favorite, "Tuesday Siesta," a woman and her daughter, both dressed in black, get off the train during the heat of the day and ask the priest for permission to visit the cemetery. At first the priest resists, because it is siesta time, but her quiet dignity prevails. In answer to the priest's queries, she states, with her had held high, that she wants to visit her son, who was shot last week for being a thief. The contrast between the ineffectual priest and the proud woman is at its peak when he pompously asks her whether she ever tried to get him on the right track:

"He was a very good man."

The priest looked first at the woman and then at the girl, and realized with a kind of pious amazement that they were not about to cry. The woman continued in the same tone:

"I told him never to steal anything that anyone needed to eat, and he minded me" (95).

The author tells us that his stories often begin with a visual image rather than an idea. He mentions this story as an example, and it is indeed a convincing one. If his early stories were perhaps too metaphysical, the later collections show a certain influence of his growing interest and experience in film, and more success in capturing certain feelings and sensations. In "One of These Days" the overwhelming sensation is that of a toothache, set against the backdrop of the wars. It is an episode which appears in a somewhat different version in *In Evil Hour*. In the story the dentist is a courageous partisan on the wrong side. But the balance of power is shifted as a result of the mayor's devastating toothache. He orders the dentist to extract it or be shot. The dentist extracts it without anesthesia, with the words: "Now you'll pay for our twenty dead men" (101). The balance of power returns to its earlier status as the dentist sarcastically asks whether to send the bill to the town or to the mayor. "It's the same damn thing" (102) is the mayor's succinct, and accurate, reply. The war and civil repression are skillfully understated, or unstated, in the reaction of the child to the mayor's threat to shoot his father: he registers neither fear nor surprise, so accustomed is he to the violence of the status quo.

"There Are No Thieves in This Town" reminds the reader of Spanish literature of a story by nineteenth-cen-

tury Valencian novelist Vicente Blasco Ibáñez, "El hal-
lazgo" ("The Windfall"), in which a thief hurriedly grabs
a pile of quilts from his victims' house, only to find an
infant inside when he arrives at home.[4] His heart goes
out to the child, and he returns it to the home, but by
now it has gotten late and the family catches him. He
goes to jail. The thief in García Márquez's story steals
billiard balls, not a child, but he finds himself in a similar
situation: what can he do with them? At first he hides
them. The whole town is talking about the theft, and a
victim is found to blame. Since the townspeople don't
want to believe it was one of them, they accuse a black
man who is passing through. The thief still holds his
tongue, but since the town's only recreation was the billiard table, he finally decides to return the balls. The
owner accuses him of stealing money as well and takes
him to the mayor, "not so much for being a thief as for
being a fool" (138). The power of gossip, so central to *In
Evil Hour,* is an interesting part of this story. When the
thief and his wife go to find out what is being said in the
town, they are almost convinced of the townspeople's
version of the events, because the people tell what they
heard with such conviction.

"Balthazar's Marvelous Afternoon" is the triumph of
the nobility of a poor man over the meanness of a rich
man, and at the same time of art over political power.
Balthazar's beautiful cage, which needs no birds for it
could sing by itself, was made with little Pepe Montiel in
mind, and cannot be sold to anyone else, even when
Pepe's father refuses to pay for it. José Montiel's anger
at the construction of the cage for his son is heightened
by Balthazar's generosity in giving it to Pepe. Balthazar

111

can't bear the child's tantrum, whereas the father doesn't seem to be affected. José Montiel, however, perceives the gift as a threat to his authority and throws the carpenter out. That the cage had been constructed, that he had not been paid for it, and that he had left it behind do not seem important to Balthazar, until he goes to the bar and sees that the supposed sale is important for his peers, who are delighted at the thought of anyone extracting money from Montiel. Balthazar can't bear to let them down, so when they buy him a beer, he buys rounds for everyone. Since the carpenter is unused to the consumption of alcohol, the festivities excite his dream to build thousands of other cages, selling them all to rich people. His understanding of rich people, from what he has seen, is that they all have ugly and contentious wives, and that they are so unhealthy that they can't even get mad, and that they're all about to die, so he must hurry up with his plans to build cages to sell them. Dead drunk but still clinging to his dream at the end, he realizes that his shoes are being taken, but he doesn't want to break the spell of the happiest dream of his life.

But José Montiel does get mad, and dies from it. His widow is the only person in town in "Montiel's Widow" who believes he has died of natural causes. So hated is this usurper of people's land that everyone expected him to die from a bullet in the back. The story explores the widow's world of unreality, and how she benefits from his despotism without knowing what is going on. While Montiel murders his poor enemies and runs the rich ones out of town so he can steal their belongings, she sympathizes with the victims. She believes her husband has helped those who had to flee, and chastises him for helping them, since they won't remember him for it. Since her premise is wrong—that her husband helped them—her conclusion is wrong. They will certainly remember him. The usurped lands are in danger of being taken by others when Montiel is no longer around, but the widow is oblivious to everything, never having been in touch with reality. She urges her children to stay in Europe, and the only time she smiles is when she receives a letter from her daughter describing the pink pigs in the butcher shops of Paris: "At the end of the letter, a hand different from her daughter's had added, "Imagine! They put the biggest and prettiest carnation in the pig's ass" (158). She only wants to stop living. It is Big Mama, in whose house she lives, who tells her in a dream that she will die when the tiredness starts in her arm.

"One Day after Saturday" paints the elderly Father Antonio Isabel as a totally methodical man, always absorbed in the temptations of the senses and how to make sermons out of them, a man who connects the dead birds in the town, not with the record-breaking heat, but with the Apocalypse. He has never been able to persuade the equally aged widow Rebeca to reveal to him the mysterious circumstances of her husband's death years before. When Father Antonio Isabel takes a dying bird into her house, he seems to fear her concupiscence more than the suspicions that she is a murderer. The birds cause his Sunday sermon to turn to the appearance of the Wandering Jew, and when he collects money to fight off the terrible apparition, he gives it to the poor young man who has just arrived in the town, seeking his mother's pension. In his mind's wanderings he believes that maybe it is possible to be happy, if only it weren't so hot.

"Artificial Roses" shows the intergenerational tensions in a family as a result of repression and hypocrisy. The roses Mina makes and her false sleeves are as unreal as the appearances she must keep up. Her blind grandmother sees better than anyone into Mina's reality, but only to try to control her behavior. In a comment on madness, which García Márquez deals with in depth in *One Hundred Years of Solitude,* this story shows the lucid grandmother as crazy, but as she says herself, "Apparently you haven't thought of sending me to the madhouse so long as I don't start throwing stones" (197).

The title story in this collection, "Big Mama's Funeral," is the first example of an accumulation of hyperbole, a technique García Márquez uses extremely well here and in later works. An enumeration of Big Mama's properties and powers is endless and fanciful, including a brilliant collection of set phrases particularly from the field of journalism. When she dies, it hadn't occurred to anyone to think she was mortal. In a way she is the prototype of the patriarch to come, though her power is inherited from her family, and kept in part because she never married. Matriarch of everyone and "well enough endowed by Nature to suckle her whole issue all by herself, [she] was dying a virgin and childless" (205).

The narrator who tells the whole story in all its details sees his role as protector of the truth against distortions and memory loss, and he is anxious to do so before the historians get hold of it and before the garbage men sweep up the garbage from the funeral forever. This grand funeral is to be attended by the pope, for Big Mama died in the odor of sanctity.

When García Márquez wrote the story, a visit by the

pope to Colombia was unthinkable, but even so he changed the physical appearance of the President of the Republic in order not to be accused of pointing to anyone in particular. But by the time the real pope came to Latin America, the President of the Republic fit the description in the story. Big Mama dies as a saint, or at least as much of a saint as the mother of the patriarch, Bendición Alvarado, whom he tries to have canonized. Both Bendición and Big Mama also come almost full circle chronologically, since they are presented after their deaths as young women again. In the case of Big Mama, a photograph of her when she was twenty-two and the printed word make her instantly famous even among those who had never seen her. Big Mama had been more powerful than even the government; her secret estate includes forged electoral certificates. A patriotic hero as well as a saint, she is given the honors due a soldier killed in battle. Big Mama had melted into her own legend.

In Evil Hour

In *In Evil Hour* the medium becomes the message, as Marshall McLuhan would have it. For it is not the accusations, or rumors, in the lampoons that terrorize the town, but the fact that they make public, and put in writing, what people want to conceal. Again and again characters are heard to say that the lampoons only say what everyone already knows—for example, that Raquel Contreras's trips to get her dentures fixed were really for an abortion. What everyone believes is usually true, but not always: the alleged affair between the musician Pastor and Rosario Montero, which costs Pastor his life in the opening scene, is later debunked when the secret comes out that he was engaged to someone else. One of the few secrets kept in the town, then, turns out to be one that should have been let out. The accusation against Rebeca Asís is never clarified. Her mother-in-law defends her, saying that the child whose paternity is questioned indeed looks like an Asís, and that one shouldn't take the lampoons so seriously.

Throughout the book there are those who wish to suppress the lampoons and those who wish to ignore them. Obviously the most "decent" families have the most to fear, and it is the Asís widow who heads up the delegation to ask Father Angel to preach against them in church next Sunday. His hesitation is to cost him his job, for the widow of Asís asks for his removal as a result; those of her class must be able to count on support of the church.

The most worried people react by leaving town, and indeed someone jokes that they'll soon have to rent people from other towns. The dentist's wife is ready to abandon the town, and he points out the irony that as a member of the opposition they had tried unsuccessfully to remove him with bullets, and now she was willing to go because of some papers.

The incident points to the importance and power of the lampoons, which clearly represent literature. The mayor is unable to control them, even after he sets up a curfew and sends out patrols; the move brings people to the conclusion that the patrols themselves must be putting up the insidious posters. A woman is arrested; still the posters continue. The mayor asks Casandra, the mirror into the future, who is putting them up, and she responds with much greater irony, paradox, and subtlety than the inhabitants of Lope de Vega's collectively guilty town of Fuenteovejuna: "It's the whole town and it's nobody.' "[5]

The lampoons contain advice as well as secrets. The mayor himself does not escape. The reaction to his patrols, manned by three thugs and bound to be totally useless, appears thus: "Don't waste gunpowder on buzzards, Lieutenant" (142). The sentence indeed could have been pronounced by just about anyone in town.

There is another kind of literature even more dangerous to the powers that be than the lampoons: clandestine literature of the type we have seen in *No One Writes to the Colonel*. Because they attack the government by offering different versions of the official story, these papers pose a greater threat than barbs directed against individiuals, no matter how powerful. And so it is that the person arrested for distributing clandestine literature, Pepe Amador, is accused of putting up the lampoons. He dies at the hands of the police, and the mayor, having buried him in the police yard, uses the worn-out excuse that he has escaped. But by the next day everyone knows that he died in the same unspeakably brutal way as Don Sabas's donkeys did, according to the lampoons.

The novel, inevitably, is about power, and the mayor is an interesting case study. Having arrived in town with a patched-together suitcase, authorization to take over from the party in power, and three hired assassins, he quickly assumes control. As soon as it is established, he tries to maintain this control without violence, depending on threats in a sort of local cold war. He uses it to accumulate riches, which in turn increase his power. Having to use violence against the anarchy of the lampoons and clandestine literature shows a weakening, as the lampoon about the buzzards indicates. The incident about the toothache, in a different version here than in "One of These Days," shows a momentary relaxation of his power when the opposition dentist has the upper hand. In the novel the mayor shows up with three armed guards, and his moment of powerlessness lasts only the second of his greatest pain, etched on his memory forever in conjunction with the moisture marks he is looking at on the ceiling.

With the other powerful figure in the town, José Montiel, already dead when the novel begins, the mayor has few rivals for his land-grabbing schemes. Don Sabas is near death himself, though he continues to steal Montiel's cattle. Judge Arcadio is mostly interested in drinking beer and making love three times a night. The judge is a necessary accomplice when papers have to be signed, but he has no reason not to cooperate until Pepe Amador gets killed, and then he disappears. Father Angel has little authority, moral or otherwise; he is unable to persuade the judge's woman to legalize her situation by marrying, and since she does everything openly, she has no fear of the lampoons. Nor can he bring himself to preach against the lampoons. He can't even keep people from going to forbidden movies; they simply go to the other door where he can't see them enter. The doctor and his wife, with their European tastes in literature, command a certain respect, but they live in constant fear themselves as members of the other side. Mr. Carmichael is a rather special case. As representative of Montiel's estate, his job is to try to keep things together for the widow, but he can't get her interested in the administration of it. He does the best he can, which is not giving in to the mayor's schemes, and he spends time in jail for his trouble. But finally the mayor finds a way to make them partners, and Carmichael's dignified if somewhat exaggerated loyalty loses its reason to be. He has always striven for impartiality, as he explains to the barber, since he has eleven children to feed.

The atmosphere of terror is once again pervasive in this novel. When the movie theater owner goes to see the priest, Father Angel is surprised to see that the bulge in the enterpreneur's pocket is a flashlight and not a gun. Ironically, one of the few movies that would have been allowed by the church is about war, as if that would be a novelty for the townspeople. But it is the barber, speaking to Judge Arcadio, who makes us feel his everyday fear: " 'You don't know what it's like,' he said, 'getting up every morning with the certainty that they're going to kill you and ten years pass without their killing you' " (156).

And once again, to García Márquez it is the atmosphere that matters. At the end of the novel we're right back where we started, in the author's characteristic circularity: just as the book opened with the priest's helper giggling nervously about the appearance of the lampoons, it ends with the new helper smiling nervously about their continuation in spite of everything. Time warps range from the fantastic detective story puzzle in which a man arrives at a hotel at ten at night, but his rotting body is discovered the next morning and the autopsy shows he had been dead for a week. The judge explains to his secretary that the story is twelve years old, "but the clue had been given by Heraclitus, five centuries before Christ" (26). The priest also wonders if any time has passed since he arrived in town nineteen years ago. A much more practical, down-to-earth episode is that in which the doctor tells the judge that the only cure for his headache is not to have drunk anything the night before.

In Evil Hour was published in 1962, but the author was forced to disclaim it as a result of editorial tampering. In a supreme twist of irony, two incidents of censorship led to this rejection by García Márquez. First, a moralist who might have been one of the characters in the book decided to suppress two words he found offensive: "masturbate" and "condom." Second, a neocolonial editor in Madrid, whom the European-worshipers among the townspeople might find quite correct, took it upon himself to make the language more acceptable to a Spanish audience. The book was not republished in its original form until 1966, in Mexico, with the folllowing statement by the author:

> The first time *In Evil Hour* was published in 1962, a proofreader allowed himself to change certain terms and clean up the style, in the name of purity of language. On this occasion, the author, in his turn, has allowed himself to restore the idiomatic mistakes and stylistic barbarisms, in the name of his sovereign and arbitrary will.[6]

Innocent Eréndira and Other Stories

Two of the stories in the original Spanish *Innocent Eréndira* collection have subtitles indicating that they were written for children. Both "Un señor muy viejo con unas alas enormes" ("A Very Old Man with Enormous Wings") and "El ahogado más hermoso del mundo" ("The Handsomest Drowned Man in the World") feature adults with whom children can play, as if they were toys. In both cases, however, other adults in the story end up doing most of the playing with these bizarre humanoids. The very old man who falls to earth is thought to be an angel by some, including the wise woman of the town.[7] But he is treated more as a circus freak, and his hosts, Pelayo and Elisenda, make a fortune charging people to see him. The townspeople's suggestions about what to do with him indicate their typical viewpoints: the simplest want to name him mayor of the world, sterner ones think he should be a five-star general, and visionaries feel he should be put out to stud. Father Gonzaga is put off by the creature's inability to speak Latin, but still indecisive, he writes to Rome for instructions. The miracles the angel supposedly performs are as disoriented as he is himself: the blind man doesn't recover his sight but grows new teeth; the paralytic still can't walk but wins the lottery; and the leper's sores sprout sunflowers. In reality the angel's most salient virtues are passivity and patience. He just wants to get as comfortable as possible, get rid of the insects in his wings, and eat eggplant mush. It is only when the circus comes to town with its own freaks that the attention is diverted, and time passes imperceptibly as the angel regains his strength. He is little more than a nuisance when, having recuperated enough to fly, he waits for the wind and the light to be right and becomes "an imaginary dot on the horizon" (167).

The other strange visitor found by children is Esteban,

"the world's handsomest drowned man." They play with him until the adults take over, astonished at his size, beauty, and pride. While the men go to neighboring villages seeking clues to his identity, the women fall in love with him. They try to make clothes for him, but everything is too small; his inner strength even bursts the buttons on his clothing. Delighted that no family can be found to claim him, they adopt him, giving him a mother and a father and a place to come back to in his posthumous travels. For of course they must bury him, sending him back where he came from: the sea.

His personality also allows them to name him. He cannot be Lautaro, as some of the younger women wanted; he must be Esteban. In death as in life, he doesn't know what to do with his oversized body, and spends most of his time trying to stay out of everyone's way. The only clue about his identity is that the vegetation growing on him is from deep, faraway water, lending support to their adoption of him.

In this story García Márquez dabbles with the technique, later developed in *The Autumn of the Patriarch,* of shifting the narrator and point of view within a single line, tracing, for example, the dialogue between a nervous hostess looking for her strongest chair and an uneasy Esteban trying to avoid embarrassment. Esteban leaves behind his memory for the townspeople, along with the gifts of beauty, generosity, hope, and solidarity his visit inspired in them.

The oldest story in the collection, "El mar del tiempo perdido" ("The Sea of Lost Time"), also involves an underwater adventure. Mr. Herbert and Tobías are alive, but during their voyage they meet many dead people, some who had been there a very long time and had finally reached a state of repose.

When the smell of roses invades the town, Jacob's wife takes it as a premonition of death and asks to be buried alive. She dreads the usual mode of burial in the town: being thrown off the cliffs into the sea. Actually, the smell forebodes the arrival of Mr. Herbert, the gringo who exploits the town under the guise of charity. He arrives with all kinds of promises and trunks full of money, which his Protestant ethic won't allow him to give away without some kind of performance in return. Not unlike the foreign companies he represents, he leaves with much more than he came with. In a panorama of time the sea with its dead people is the past; the town with its unnatural smell of roses is the present; and Mr. Herbert's description of glass houses is the only vision of the future.

"Muerte constante más allá del amor" ("Death Constant Beyond Love") is a delicious political satire which appears as a story in the collection, but is incorporated into the *Innocent Eréndira* film as an episode in which Eréndira visits Senator Onésimo Sánchez. In the story the senator and the situation are the same, but the protagonist is not Eréndira but Laura Farina.[8] The favor she wants is papers legalizing her father's presence in the country, and of course her proposed method of payment is inexorably the same. The difficulty is that her father has locked up her private parts in some sort of chastity belt, to which only he has the key. The senator's demise is exactly as predicted, with him raging at dying without her.

The senator's reelection campaign techniques show

him for the phony he is; he parades cardboard buildings and even an ocean liner through town. But he also speaks the truth to his supporters: his election is just as important to them as to him, for they live on his power. Shown as a cheap politician building dependencies on himself, he is a possible version of the patriarch in his early days. Nelson Farina, Laura's father, recognizes him for what he is: "le Blacamén [sic] de la politique."[9]

He is referring to the two opposing characters in another story, "Blacamán el bueno vendedor de milagros" ("Blacamán the Good, Vendor of Miracles"). The narrator claims for himself the epithet "the Good" and refers to his employer as "the Bad." In fact, both Blacamáns are rogues totally without scruples in their dealings with the public and fiendishly cruel to each other. The Bad hires the Good to aid him as a swindler because of his foolish face, very helpful in his trade of selling all manner of deceitful merchandise with proclaimed magical properties to the unwary. After a sadistic torture scene the Good acquires magical properties and takes his revenge, which consists of reviving his dead mentor to live forever within his grave.

Like "The Handsomest Drowned Man in the World," "Blacamán" uses long sentences within which can be found shifting narrators with their necessarily changing speech patterns and identifying tags.

A barb at the viceroys is not lacking in this pungent story, as Blacamán's embalming technique makes them govern better dead than when they were alive; the marines, too, come in for attack. Fooled by Blacamán's elixirs, they take after him, killing everyone in their paths, "not only the natives, out of precaution, but also the Chinese, for distraction, the Negroes, from habit, and the Hindus, because they were snake charmers" (177).

The story that develops the shifting narrative technique to the fullest in this collection is "El último viaje del buque fantasma" ("The Last Voyage of the Ghost Ship"). Again the narrator is a young man. His goal in life, once he has seen the fabulous, immense liner, is to prove its existence to others, thereby affirming his worth. At sea in his little boat, he spots the ship during the intervals when the beam from the lighthouse is not shining on it, for it disappears with the flash of light. Both Sir Francis Drake and William Dampier make their way into this story, representing death and fear, respectively. The narrator's obsession absorbs the reader with the appearance, once a year on a Wednesday in March, of the phantasmagoric vessel until, to prove his version of reality, he leads the ship to crash in the port as he shouts, "There it is, you cowards, a second before the huge steel cask shattered the ground and one could hear the neat destruction of ninety thousand five hundred champagne glasses breaking, one after the other, from stem to stern" (194). The story, like the last section of *The Autumn of the Patriarch,* is told in a single sentence, and is replete with striking visual imagery, mostly related to the sea,—for example, the "lovemaking of manta rays in a springtime of sponges" (189).

Something of a folk tale with its engagingly long title, its monstrous grandmother with green blood, and the charming, angelic hero Ulises, "The Incredible and Sad Tale of Innocent Eréndira and Her Heartless Grandmother" blends legend, myth, allegory, and previous literature into its rich tapestry. Though all four elements of the universe that fascinated medieval readers are evident—the sea as water, the desert as earth, the fire that twice dooms Eréndira—it is the presence of the wind that overwhelms. From the very first line, when the "wind of her misfortune began to blow," (1), it is connected with Eréndira's fate. The missionaries capture her while a wind almost as fierce is blowing, treating Eréndira to a shift in her history of exploitation from her grandmother to the church. The wind of her misfortune blows again before her fateful attempt to escape with the hapless Ulises, and finally she runs into the wind of the desert, never to be heard from again. The photographer too is subject to the wind, and in fact travels wherever it takes him.

The subjection to nature, specifically the wind, parallels Eréndira's maddeningly passive acceptance of her fate. She is treated as a virtual slave by her grandmother from earliest childhood, and the exploitation of prostitution is merely added on to her other tasks. Her trip to the convent breaks, at least for a time, the endless parade of men waiting for her favors, but her duties within the walls consist of whitewashing the stairs every time anyone goes up or down them. When Grandmother finally devises a way of getting her back, Eréndira has her moment to speak but returns, inevitably, to her. In fact, rebelling doesn't occur to her until Grandmother herself, albeit unwittingly, suggests it; before Grandmother's monologue envisioning Eréndira's future life without her, that possibility hadn't crossed the girl's mind. Afterward it obsesses her. Unable to murder the old lady herself, she enlists the help of her hero, Ulises.

But Ulises is really not much of a hero, and at first the

great lady is too much for him. Eréndira is impatient with his failed attempts, and when he succeeds, his painful shouts are more those of a son than of a lover, and Eréndira is gone, forever, with the gold. Eréndira, seeing the face of her dead grandmother, has attained the maturity that eluded her during the twenty years of her misfortune.

Grandmother is a total exploiter, with no redeeming value, not only of Eréndira but of everyone. As if she were running a company store, she deducts so much from the Indians who work for her that they have hardly anything left. She settles accounts with the musicians by her sleight-of-hand figuring, having them play two happy numbers for every waltz, to avoid paying them what she already owes them. She wants the photographer to pay for the music too, even though, as he points out, it doesn't come out in the pictures. She argues with him that it isn't fair to have a poor innocent child paying for everything. Indeed.

Her unremitting evil underscores the irony of her having to get a letter of recommendation for her good character, for the person she gets it from is every bit as degenerate as herself, the very Senator Onésimo Sánchez. The letter serves its purpose even though the policeman she shows it to when she needs to recapture Eréndira can't read.

Eréndira has few happy moments. When she first hears music, during her stay in the convent, she knows happiness perhaps for the first time. It is not enough to keep her inside, but perhaps it offsets the endless whitewashing of the stairs. The truck loader treats her with tenderness instead of the brutality she is accustomed to, and she makes love with him willingly. But it is Ulises who first makes her laugh. She is charmed, she says, by the serious way the golden lad talks about nonsense. Indeed it seems like nonsense to readers as well as to Eréndira that his father's oranges might be worth 50,000 pesos each, but that is before we find out that each one contains a large diamond. In this exchange, García Márquez might be showing his own penchant for saying outrageous things with deadpan straight delivery, a characteristic, he claims, that he learned from his grandmother and to which he attributes a measure of his success as a storyteller.

One must accuse him of exaggeration only with great caution, however. Clearly he's having great fun at the expense of the mayor, whose job consists of shooting clouds to make it rain. But the *Wall Street Journal* of 6 August 1985 ran a story about Spanish farmers who are convinced that it is sinister planes that come and attack their thunderclouds, keeping them from raining on their parched fields.

The church comes under attack as well, along with its intransigent representatives from the Iberian Peninsula. Just as the priest in *In Evil Hour* argued with the judge's woman that she should marry now to legitimize the child she will have, the priests search the highways, byways, and remotest villages for pregnant Indian women to persuade or force them to marry. The resistance is always for the same reason: they receive better treatment as concubines than as wives. But they finally succumb, usually to treachery or a pair of flashy earrings.

The depiction of the lack of communication within marriage is wryly humorous as well. Ulises's father is

Dutch, his mother Indian. Each speaks to him in her or his language and wants to know what the other has said, to which Ulises's usual response seems to be "Nothing special."

Though nearly the entire story is told in third-person narration, García Márquez indulges in a curious example of first-person intrusion into the text, the details of which are accurately autobiographical. Just after the unsuccessful escape attempt the author begins to tell the story himself, explaining that it was at that point in time that he knew the protagonists. It would not be until much later, however, that he would tell the tale, inspired by the singer Rafael Escalona, who composed one of his pieces about them. Saying that he was there to sell encyclopedias, the narrator blends back into the atmosphere of their greatest splendor, when they attracted the circus with its Blacamán, its girl who had been transformed into a spider for disobeying her parents, and its announcement of the arrival of the astral bat.

Innocent Eréndira was originally composed as a filmscript. Brilliantly directed in Mexico by Brazilian Ruy Guerra and starring Irene Pappas as the monstrous grandmother, Claudia Ohana as Eréndira, and Michel Lonsdale as Ulises, the film captures visually some of the images García Márquez makes us conjure up in our minds. Particularly striking is the episode of the enamored Ulises changing the color of glass he touches. The shots of the desert and the sea point to their similarities, as Ulises had explained. The wind is absolutely pervasive. Onésimo Sánchez's phoniness is emphasized by his election poster in the film, reading "Onésimo es distinto" (Onésimo is different). According to Eréndira, that slogan backfires, for people know exactly what to expect from the politicians they are used to, who are all alike.

There are a couple of slight changes that work better in the story. The relationship between the music and Eréndira's happiness is not very clear in the film but very effective in the novella; the contraband pearls are much more exotic than the watches Eréndira pulls out of the sacks of grain. But on the whole, each medium convinces in its way and both are successful. The film has few special effects; the one episode of Eréndira's hand acquiring its lines as a sign of her maturity, freedom from her grandmother, and being for the first time in charge of her own destiny is effective in the film and absent from the book, though it is a factor, as we have seen, in *The Autumn of the Patriarch*.

With the exception of the very earliest stories, all García Márquez's works usually considered minor are characterized by their very visual imagery. One can easily believe him when he states that his stories usually start with an image in the mind's eye, and can appreciate the influence film has had on his fiction. Some critics have said that all the early works are understudies, sketches, or outlines for the masterpiece that follows, but each taken separately has its own special quality, and taken together these early works form an impressive body of literature.

NOTES

1. *Leaf Storm and Other Stories* (New York: Avon, 1972) 106, includes stories from other collections, notably *La increíble y triste historia de la cándida Eréndira y de su abuela desalmada.* I will use this edition for all quotations from the novella and from the other stories appearing with it. For a listing of the stories in all Spanish and English collections see the bibliography.

2. This episode is related by Oscar Collazos in *García Márquez. La soledad y la gloria; Su vida y obra.* (Barcelona: Plaza y Janes, 1983) 52.

3. *No One Writes to the Colonel and Other Stories* (New York: Avon, 1968) 32. Quotations from the novella and the other stories included, which form the entirety of the Big Mama's Funeral collection, will be from this edition.

4. "The Windfall" appears in Ibáñez, *The Last Lion and Other Tales* (Boston: John W. Luce, 1919).

5. *In Evil Hour* (New York: Avon, 1980) 133. All quotations are from this paperback edition.

6. *La mala hora* (Mexico: Era, 1966); my translation.

7. Certain peculiarities in the translation of this story were noticed by Vera M. Kutinski in "The Logic of Wings: Gabriel García Márquez and Afro-American Literature," *Latin American Literary Review* 13, (1985): 133–46. Apparently trying to universalize certain local features, Gregory Rabassa uses the word *earth* instead of *Caribbean* and *Portuguese* instead of *Jamaican,* for example.

8. The title and theme of this story form an interesting homage to Spanish Golden Age poet Francisco de Quevedo, reversing the meaning of sonnet 471, "Amor constante más allá de la muerte," which speaks of love beyond the grave.

9. The English version of *Innocent Eréndira and Other Stories* (New York: Harper, 1979) 87, contains only two of the short stories—that appeared originally with the novella. Quotations from those stories and "Innocent Eréndira" will be from this edition. See note 1 and the primary bibliography.

CHAPTER FIVE

Story and History:
Journalism and Fiction

An etymological dictionary will reveal that "history" and "story" have the same root, and students of Romance languages will have noticed that there is still only one word for the two related terms in English. *Webster's New Twentieth Century Dictionary* defines history as "an account of what has happened; narrative; story; tale" as its first definition; the word *story* is "the telling of a happening or connected series of happenings, whether true or fictitious; an account; a narration." Further down the list of possible meanings are two interesting uses in English of *story:* a falsehood; a fib. [colloq.] and history [archaic]." A curious turn of language indeed, that begins with something assumed to be true and ends up with a usage that indicates the opposite.

Journalism has its own use for the word *story,* which works on the assumption that the account called a "story" is true. García Márquez's earliest journalism, as well as his later novelistic preoccupations, show a keen interest in getting at a truth beyond bare-boned facts, which can, of course, be used to misrepresent the truth in a larger context. Some critics have called him anti-intellectual and anti-science; in my view he is neither, but he is suspicious of and hostile to an overrational interpretation of the world. His purpose in writing is to explore a larger truth, and to force his readers to consider extrarational modes of perception.

This characteristic of his work has been apparent from pieces he wrote as early as the late 1940s and early 1950s. In an article published in 1950 he criticizes the so-called progress of science in a world that is becoming increasingly dependent on its specialized and partial visions. Until someone proclaimed that the world was round, he declares, a poetic vision was recognized as valid too. The example is particularly important in view of his later creation of José Arcadio Buendía, whose scientific explorations seem always to be wrongheaded, not because the information is incorrect, but because his interpretation is too narrow. José Arcadio does not confine his curiosity to scientific knowledge; he also explores alchemy. But he doesn't follow its rules closely enough, and he never integrates the different forms of knowledge at his disposal.

In his indefatigable search for alternatives to the official story García Márquez seems fascinated with new light shed on old sources. In 1950 he wrote a news story about a certain Dr. Guido Kirch in New York who discovered in ancient parchments that Adam and Eve had a daughter named Naoba. The source was said to be nine hundred years old. Such a manuscript seems ancient to us, of course, but in relation to the events it describes it becomes one of those efforts to reconstruct a happening in the past based on far less testimony than the "shards of memory" García Márquez evokes in *Chronicle of a Death Foretold*. The story is another example of ideas that were to appear in later fiction. Both the manuscripts and the Bible find their way into not only *One Hundred Years of Solitude* but several other narrations as well.

García Márquez's early work as a journalist deserves much more study than it has received.[1] It includes many items of short fiction as well as musings on political events of the day; film reviews; imitations of Kafka, who fascinated him at the time; treatises on nightmares, insanity, and death; and of course a healthy skepticism of too much dependence on rationality. In a fiction series referred to as the Marquesa stories he continues the enchanting tales of a groom who sends exotic gifts to his bride even after he feels the relationship should be ended, because the author can't bring himself to terminate these interesting characters. The author explains his problem to his character in a letter to her, reminiscent of Miguel de Unamuno's conversation with the protagonist of *Niebla,* Augusto Pérez.

Time is never far away from his thoughts, and in a respectfully humorous elegy for George Bernard Shaw, he congratulates the Irish writer on his good sense of timing, having died on All Souls Day. In another elegy, for Ernest Hemingway, García Márquez masterfully and ironically evokes the opening pages of *Death in the Afternoon* in its title: "Dead From Natural Causes." Politics too is in the forefront, and some of his most interesting pieces are the result of his trip though the Eastern European countries during his first stay in Europe. As he matures, his interest in politics becomes much more sophisticated, and he never stops making acute observations about world politics with a formidable storehouse of information about different parts of the world.

The Story of a Shipwrecked Sailor

Some of García Márquez's most intriguing work falls somewhere in between the strictly defined categories of fiction and journalism. *The Story of a Shipwrecked Sailor* first appeared serially in *El Espectador* in 1955. It is the hallucinatory tale of a sailor who was washed off the deck of his navy destroyer in heavy seas and survived aboard a life raft for ten days without food or water before swimming ashore on the Colombian coast in a sparsely populated area. The series was presented as news and interspersed with other news items. But in the republication of the piece as a book in 1970 García Márquez claims his own voice as well as the sailor's, and rightly so, when he refers to the story as a "journalistic reconstruction" of what the sailor told him in lengthy interviews. Indeed, the voice of García Márquez is apparent throughout, especially in the prologue, which he calls "The Story of the Story." No one would miss the sarcasm of his description of the function of the U.S. Panama Canal Authority as the performance of "military and other humanitarian deeds in the Southern Caribbean." What he didn't know when he started the story was that there was a scandal behind the accident, covered up by the Colombian government. The first news stories reported that the mishap was due to a storm, but the sailor, Luis Alejandro Velasco, surprised García Márquez with the revelation that there was no storm. A check of weather charts confirmed his assertion. The ship had nearly capsized, throwing off eight crew members, because it was carrying heavy and ill-secured contraband. Velasco was virtually sequestered by the Colombian navy to prevent him talking to reporters until much later, after he had profited from his story by doing commercials advertising his watch, which never stopped, and his shoes, which were so tough he couldn't take them apart to chew on.

Because of these commercials, when Velasco first presented himself to the offices of García Márquez's newspaper, no one was interested in his story. The editor changed his mind and had his reporter do the interviews. The writer's interest was pricked when he realized what a good storyteller Velasco was, and what a precise memory he had. Still, perhaps the greatest danger in such a story is that of tedium. The artistry with which this pitfall is avoided is the work of genius; in a carefully structured narration in the first person, each day is marked by a specific event that keeps it separate from the other days. Even so, in an episode that must have fascinated the author, Velasco at one point loses track of both time and space. Since he can see nothing but the sea, he loses all spatial orientation and cannot tell whether the raft has turned around or in which direction he is heading. Likewise, he becomes confused by the passage of time, particularly since the accident took place on February 28 and he isn't sure which day is the first of March. Aware that this doesn't matter as much as how many days he has actually been on the raft, he realizes he can't tell that for sure either. Toward the end, when he wakes and sees a feeble light, he isn't sure whether it is dawn or sunset.

The use of detail is masterful. At first, time is of utmost importance. Velasco sees that the whole tragedy took place within ten minutes. Believing he will be rescued immediately, he can't understand why they are taking so long. He knows exactly when the ship was to arrive in Cartagena. As he is washed off the deck, the ship seems suspended in air, then disappears. He notices that daybreak is much faster on the water than on land. The most excruciating moments are those when the sharks appear, punctually at five in the evening every day.

Velasco finally sights land and swims ashore. His greatest surprise is that the people who find him know nothing of the accident. Yet within hours he has become a kind of circus freak, and by the time he goes to the town with a doctor, he is accompanied by six hundred people, virtually the entire town. He suspects that someone is selling tickets to get a glance of him, as would later be the case in García Márquez's fanciful story "A Very Old Man with Enormous Wings."

The story is a kind of journalism that stresses entertainment rather than information. Using exact times and many details of the actual events, the author creates a story that holds the interest of the reader well beyond the gathering of data. García Márquez will turn to pure fiction in his next works. But he will never leave journalism behind, as he continues to write both newspaper articles and some intriguing works that fall somewhere in between the genres.

Chronicle of a Death Foretold

After the tremendous success of *One Hundred Years of Solitude* and the experimental techniques of *The Autumn of the Patriarch,* García Márquez returned to journalism in a most original way. For *Chronicle of a Death Foretold* is a novel, but one in which the vision of a journalist is paramount. Based on an occurrence in the Colombian town of Sucre in 1951, it is a tale of lost and violently regained honor. The author lived in Sucre at the time, and was a friend of the families of both the victim and the executioners. Nearly thirty years after the events García Márquez returned to the scene, took testimonies from the principal actors and many witnesses, and reconstructed the story as would an investigative reporter. He also pored through the poorly kept official records of the trial, including marginal remarks of the presiding judge.

Two things intrigued the author about this tragedy: the doubt about whether Santiago Nasar was indeed the despoiler of Angela Vicario's virginity, and the fact that her twin brothers very obviously did not want to take the prescribed revenge against the accused perpetrator, who was their friend. Only Angela Vicario knows whether he really deflowered her, and the person on whom she is based, a cousin of García Márquez, has always stood by her story. That the twins wanted to be stopped from the killing they didn't want to commit is obvious on nearly every page of the novel, and indeed their continual announcements of the revenge give title to it. Santiago Nasar seems the only one in town who doesn't know the threat hovering over him, and when the father of his betrothed tells him, only minutes before the crime, he is so befuddled that he can't react rationally.

The novel also has traits of the detective genre in the way it unfolds, from witness to witness, with the surmisings of the narrator throughout as he tries to put back together the "broken mirror of memory . . . from so many scattered shards."[2] In fact it is the role of the narrator that binds together the diverse elements of this novel. For the narrator is García Márquez himself, clearly identified several times as a writer and journalist who returns to a town where his family lived briefly, a town marked by this tragedy for years afterward. The people he interviews in his investigation are his relatives, friends, the townspeople he knew from his youth. His own role in the events is still peripheral, however, as he unabashedly admits: "I was recovering from the wedding revels in the apostolic lap of María Alejandrina Cervantes" (4-5)—making him perhaps the only other person in the town who was not forewarned about the impending murder.

The excuses the townspeople present for not having warned the victim range from not wanting to interfere in a matter of honor to the priest's plaintive admission that he forgot. Colonel Aponte actually sees Nasar but says nothing, as do several others on the fateful morning. Some think the twins incapable of the deed, others try to get word to Nasar and fail. One who tries hardest and worries most is Clotilde Armenta, who has the milk bar across the plaza. She sends word to Victoria Guzmán, who does not deliver the message to Nasar for reasons of her own. Cristo Bedoya, intimate friend of the victim, goes as far as entering Nasar's house and even his mother's bedroom to warn them, but to no avail, for Nasar at that moment is out of the house.

The role of Nasar's mother is poignant. Known to be an interpreter of dreams, she fails to see the clear warnings in the recent dreams of her son. After she receives the warning, and believing her son to be in the house, she locks the door that is usually open and through which Santiago Nasar could have escaped his bloody fate. Years later she still sees the vision of her son in the narrator-journalist-friend who comes to see her.

The tension so pervasive in the novel comes from various sources. The reader knows from the first line that Santiago Nasar will be killed, but has to wait to find out why and how. The author feeds that information little by little, and not consistently. Eyewitness accounts are undercut by contradictions. Even on a point as neutral as the weather there can be no agreement. The unreliability of memory as well as excuses and alibis tend to color particular versions of what happened. The greatest tension throughout the book is a result of the fatalism inherent in the much-announced death in contrast with the many possibilities of escaping that fate. In this sense the role of the twins becomes so important: they feel compelled, by an outdated and absurd social system, to commit a murder. They cry out for help, but the townspeople are so immersed themselves in the antiquated and barbarous system that they cannot or will not intervene. The brothers even try to talk each other out of going through with the crime, but are unable to break out of the code of honor: "It's as if it had already happened," Pablo Vicario says impatiently to Pedro (61).

Other people in the town, knowing Santiago Nasar is going to die, see him as a ghost already but are still unable to warn him. Divina Flor knows he is a marked man, and shudders that his hand feels like that of a dead man. Clotilde Armenta sees him as a ghost as well. But one of the most striking visions/foreshadowings is that of Hortensia Baute, who sees the brothers with their knives

140

before the crime and imagines that they are already dripping with blood.

Another gruesome foreshadowing is the kitchen scene of Victoria Guzmán slaughtering rabbits and feeding the fresh guts to the dogs. Santiago protests her barbarity, unsuspecting that a similar fate awaits him in only a few moments. After the knifing, when he staggers back into the kitchen holding his intestines, the dogs are ready to devour them until Plácida Linero has them killed. In an inexorable repetition, not to say overkill, the clumsily performed autopsy makes the priest remark, "It was as if we killed him all over again after he was dead." (72). Similarly, the odor of wedding flowers prompts Santiago to confess to the narrator that he doesn't like flowers when they are closed in, for it reminds him of funerals. He concludes that he doesn't want flowers at his funeral, and of course it is less than a day later that the narrator finds himself in charge of preventing people from bringing flowers to Santiago's wake.

The star-crossed lovers in this story deserve special attention. Angela Vicario is first portrayed as being poor in spirit; she is pretty but with a helpless air. She does not want to marry Bayardo San Román; fearing the consequences of her lost virginity, she nonetheless does not have the strength to fight off her family as well as Bayardo. She gives in to the pressures. But at the moment of truth she is too honorable to go through with the Celestinesque tricks to deceive her husband and is returned to her parents. She identifies Nasar with no hesitation, nailing his name to the wall "with her well-aimed dart, like a butterfly with no will whose sentence has always been written" (47). But after the brutal beating inflicted by her scandalized mother Angela is changed forever, finally taking charge of her fate by breaking out of the hypocritical societal system. Her mother spends the rest of her life trying "to make Angela Vicario die in life" (89), but Angela lives honestly and as she wishes, talking about her life with anyone who will listen and not holding back any secrets.

Bayardo San Román is less than open, and in many ways a perfect macho. His insistence on marrying Angela is a manifestation of power; the possibility of acquiring something pretty, of winning a prized possession. His acquisition of the widower's house is similar. He decides he wants it, and nothing can stop him. A victim of deception and disappointment, he returns to his solitary and ill-gotten house to drink himself into oblivion until he is rescued by the doctor. Bayardo becomes humanized through the endless letters he receives from Angela, and in a perfect ending he shows up on her doorstep years later with a suitcase of clothes and the intention to stay with her, and another suitcase with all the unread letters she has been sending him over the years.

It is only in this episode of the happy and tidy ending that García Márquez's version of the story differs greatly from the factual account, in which the groom marries someone else and surrounds himself with a numerous family. With his references in the story to life resembling bad literature, here it seems that he insists on his right as a writer to improve things for the sake of balance, harmony, and his own version of truth. Far from a clichéd ending to a story of violence, it is an ending that closes one circle and opens others. The vision of Bayardo's homecoming, so to speak, is not that of two lovers riding off into the sunset; we can only imagine the possibilities in store for them. In his youth Bayardo San Román had a way of talking that "served to conceal rather than to reveal" (26). Might Angela's persistent writing have made him rethink some of his old values, even though he only imagines what the letters contain?

Of the brothers in the real drama García Márquez makes twins. Pedro and Pablo Vicario are identical and complementary at the same time. Pedro's stint in the service makes him the stronger of the two, and Pablo follows his orders. But Pedro has also brought disease back from the service, and it flares up just as they are about to fulfill their perceived duty. Pablo has to urge him on. It was Pedro who decided they had to kill Nasar, but he considers the honor debt fulfilled when the mayor disarmed them. Pablo assumes command in a fateful inevitability: Nasar must die, and the honor code leaves little — room for interpretation. He is simply filling in for his brother's temporary lack of resolution.

Both the epigraph and a quotation the narrator attributes to himself are taken from the sixteenth-century bilingual Portuguese writer Gil Vicente, and both warn of the pitfalls in pursuit of love, comparing it to hunting. Santiago Nasar is a hunter before he becomes the hunted, both of animals on his ranch and of all the young women in the town. Though we are told that most of the townspeople didn't believe he had made love with Angela, he had certainly pursued many others. His designs on Divina Flor may have cost him his life; if Victoria Guzmán had not despised him and wanted to protect her daughter, perhaps she would have warned him. His real passion is María Alejandrina Cervantes, and it is in rela-

tion to her that the narrator quotes the line of poetry:
"A falcon who chases a warlike crane can only hope for a
life of pain" (65). The message could be for Bayardo San
Román as well, and the choice underlines once again
García Márquez's love of poetry. Even as a journalistic
account of a bloody crime, *Chronicle of a Death Foretold*
is remarkably lyrical, close always to the pervasive
themes of love and death.

El Secuestro

In another re-creation of a historical event, *El secuestro* (The Kidnapping) recounts in the form of a documen-
tary film script the take-over of a fancy party by
Sandinistas before their triumph over Somoza in 1979.
The guests are members of Nicaragua's upper crust,
wealthy government and business people whose fates
mattered a great deal to the regime. The party-goers are
decadent but not inhuman; the members of Sandinista
Comando group called Juan José Quezada are idealistic
but very practical, tough with negotiators but humane
with their prisoners. They are identified only by numbers; the leader is Cero, and the others, including three
women, are called only by their numbers, from One to
Fifteen.

The voice of the narrator, docent but not intrusive in
the beginning, belongs to one of the members of the commando squad. The action begins in media res, with the
take-over itself, but flashbacks show the still unrepaired
scenes of destruction from the previous year's devastat-

ing earthquakes, cars full of masked people, and the house where the Sandinistas are training. They do not know each other and are not from the capital, nor do they know how to handle arms. They are shown studying the invitation list for the party and discussing plans. They prepare to leave their house, destroying all documentation of their stay there, and head for one of the poorest neoghborhoods, safe because electricity has not been restored.

Details show their careful planning and political decisions. They know the American ambassador has been invited but that he usually leaves early. Since they wish to deal directly with the Nicaraguan government without interventions, they wait until he leaves to attack the house. The only execution is that of the host, who runs to his bedroom to arm himself. In fact, his stockpile of arms impresses the Sandinistas, whose weapons are not nearly as modern, and they make good use of the windfall.

Faithful to the working classes, the rebels make every effort not to compromise its members. They pay the taxi driver the night's pay he will lose and allow some of the servants in the house to leave. They do not mistreat anyone, and in fact are indulgent with the prisoners, allowing them to have the food brought in which was ordered for the party, to make a phone call, to go for their smoking supplies and medicine.

But they are very tough, and wise, with the officials. At first they think they are talking with Somoza's half brother, but they soon find out it is the general himself. Somoza has the gall to try a repetition of the disastrous Red Cross trick which had decimated rebels in an earlier episode: the rebels had allowed in good faith Red Cross trucks filled with soldiers to enter. Now the Sandinistas' demands are clear and most are nonnegotiable: freedom for their list of prisoners, which include current President Daniel Ortega, raising salaries of workers, access to the radio station, five million dollars, and passage to Cuba.

The governmental stalling and silly excuses seem interminable and incomprehensible. Several days later, with a vision of the inside of the jail, we realize the delay was due to the poor physical condition of the tortured prisoners. The early government radio report contrasts with the reality on the screen and infuriates the Sandinistas, underscoring their insistence on access to the media.

The action in the house is interspersed with slides showing Nicaraguan history, especially during the 1930s, the epoch of Augusto Sandino. The negotiations are long and frustrating, underlining the intransigence of the government and the calloused and hypocritical attitude of the papal nuncio, who seems more interested in the monetary demand than any of the others. Finally, all demands are met except that they receive only one million dollars, and they accept after issuing detailed instructions for freeing the prisoners and themselves and transferring the money to the plane waiting to take them to Cuba.

The last scene, with shots of the tense trip to the airport, gives way to the voice of the radio announcer, who reads the tenets of the Sandinista movement. While giving the film time to show the denouement, the radio message goes on more than it needs to and becomes too didactic for a sophisticated audience, ending predictably with "Viva Sandino!" repeated several times as the plane lifts off the runway.

146

The role of this script as a history lesson is obvious. Beyond that, its greatest strength is the portrayal of characters in their interrelations, both with others on their side and with their enemies. The author favors the Sandinistas, of course, but avoids making them flawless heroes or their adversaries caricatures. The papal nuncio receives the worst treatment, but the Monseñor is shown as a gentle man who only wants to avoid bloodshed. Details show us glimpses of the others: the rich lady who swallows her expensive ring, fearful it will be taken; the constant parade to the bathroom, which Cero solves by turning a bucket into a pissoir so he can make better use of his soldiers. Within the Sandinista troops roles are still quite traditional; the women concern themselves with the distribution of food and the nursing of wounded, while of the three higher-ranking members of the commando squad, all are men. The only one who falls asleep is Fifteen, and Cero is not harsh with her for the blunder.

The book does not dwell on prison conditions, but we get a glimpse of the prisoners listening to a tiny radio, trying to figure out from the government-controlled news what is going on. As a guard approaches, they have to throw it out the window, painfully underlining both their isolation and the difficulty with which they obtained the sputtering radio.

The importance of the news, and of radios, gives occasion for one of the few humorous scenes in the script. Trying on their own to get to the radio stations, the Sandinistas call from the house directly and explain the situation to the announcers. Unfortunately, it is *el dia de los inocentes*, the equivalent of April Fool's Day, so no one believes them when they say they have taken control of the party. It seems too fantastic. Disgusted, they have to wait until the radio speech is accepted as one of their demands.

Reading *Innocent Eréndira*, which was also originally a film script, one notices its visual qualities without having to fill in descriptions, for García Márquez rewrote the piece as a novel. *El secuestro* has not been rewritten, and therefore it is not as easy to read. Somewhat hampered by stage directions such as the showing of slides, without really being able to visualize their content, the reader at times needs more detail. Nevertheless, it is a well-written story about a fascinating subject, with all the material necessary for a first-rate, action-packed, and informative film.

Clandestine in Chile

A long monologue by a filmmaker about his work may not seem the most spellbinding medium for either the filmmaker or the interviewer to tell a story, but *Clandestine in Chile: The Adventures of Miguel Littín* gives us an amazing view of the man, his work, and especially a vision of Chile under the Pinochet dictatorship which began in 1973 that in some ways surpasses the films whose production it describes. As in *The Story of a Shipwrecked Sailor*, the combination of the journalist doing the interview and the narrator in first person telling his own story dovetails perfectly to create a startling picture of ordinary as well as extraordinary lives in a country

148

whose previous democratic traditions made the brutality of repression more of shock than in less socially progressive regimes, more used to rule by strongmen not unlike the protagonist of *The Autumn of the Patriarch.*

Miguel Littín, foremost filmmaker in Chile and head of the newly nationalized Chile Films under President Allende, mentioned his fantasy of entering Chile clandestinely to make such a film, and one of his listeners took him at his word, putting him in contact with the necessary backers for such a project. Several European and Chilean film teams were involved, as well as a network of exiles and resisters within Chile.

Exiled in perpetuity by Pinochet, Littín had to change his appearance and indeed his persona to enter and stay in his country. In some ways this was the most difficult part of the job, as he transformed himself into a Uruguayan businessman, getting used to a new accent and new clothes, new gestures, and above all a new female companion, Elena, who would act as his wife and business partner.

Despite the first-person narration and a story about the actions of Miguel Littín told by himself, the voice of García Márquez is clear, as he says in the prologue, "since a writer's voice is not interchangeable." In condensing eighteen hours of tape into a text of 116 pages, the incidents he decides to choose and to emphasize become his work, just as the editing of the 100,000 feet of film into six hours of viewing is that of Littín. Throughout the tense narration one sees the structures of García Márquez and episodes that one might imagine forming part of his fiction. If the famous park created by vintner Matías Cousiño for the woman he loved, bringing in all manner of exotic flora and fauna from all over the world, didn't exist in reality, perhaps Florentino Ariza would have invented it for Fermina Daza. Littín, upon seeing a surprising number of lovers on the streets of Santiago, recalls a remark someone made to him recently in Madrid: "Love blossoms in times of the plague" (43). If the speaker wasn't García Márquez himself, it might as well have been, and particularly in view of the timing: the author worked on *Love in the Time of Cholera* at virtually the same time as this book.

Other familiar figures, situations, and turns of phrase identify the Colombian, though in his introduction he claims having tried "to keep the Chilean idioms of the original and, in all cases, to respect the narrator's way of thinking, which does not always coincide with mine." (x). Littín's mother, like García Márquez's in *Chronicle of a Death Foretold*, and like many other fictional creations of the author, has premonitions; how else to explain her preparation of *mastul*, the time-consuming Greek holiday dish that she had ready when he arrived, although it was no special holiday? The description of seafood as "prehistoric shellfish mollusks" may have been uttered by Littín, but it sounds as Marquean as the prehistoric eggs of Macondo. The code informing Littín that his Italian colleague Grazia has safely left the country is that she ascended into heaven, not unlike the fabulous uplifting of Remedios the Beauty in *One Hundred Years of Solitude*.[5] Littín is surprised when he is given an electronic chess set as a mark of his indentification in a church until he enters the church and sees people reading newspapers and novels, playing cards, knitting, or playing children's games: in the setting a chess set is the perfect cover. Just as the poorest neighborhoods were the safest place for the Sandinistas to hide in *El secuestro*, for their lack of services, so are they in Santiago, and indeed Littín compares them to the Arabic Casbahs in their labyrinthine streets, curiously free from police action. They are similar too to the dogfight district before the patriarch's visits to Manuela Sánchez transformed the neighborhood into a false image of its former self.

The most poignant section of the book for supporters of Allende and lovers of poetry is the one entitled "Two of the Dead Who Never Die: Allende and Neruda." Littín, in Valparaiso where Allende grew up, hears a woman saying that she remains an Allende supporter even now, and another say that Allende is the only president who ever spoke about women's issues. The last president's sense of humor is nostalgically recalled in the epitaph he wants on his tomb, after having been talked about as a presidential candidate many times but before actually getting elected for the job: "Here lies Salvador Allende, future president of Chile." During a political campaign Allende went down into the audience to shake the hand of a man who yelled out to him, "This is a shitty government, but it's my government" (59).

The vision of Pablo Neruda, poet of love and himself a candidate for president before he threw his support to Allende, is just as heartrending and a poem itself within the account. His place in Isla Negra, in reality neither an island nor black, may be a place where everything is prohibited, as the guard tells the film crew, but no one can stop the graffiti that continue to crop up with messages of love: "Juan and Rosa love each other through Pablo; Thank you, Pablo, for teaching us love; We want to love as much as you loved" and the more overtly political "Generals: Love never dies; Allende and Neruda live; One minute of darkness will not make us blind" (64). But the most powerful testimonial of the presence of Neruda and his love is the earth itself. Ever since the last earthquake, the land shakes every ten of fifteen minutes; hearing the creaking wood, the tinkling of metal and glass "as on a yacht adrift, ... one had the impression that the whole world was trembling with all the love sown in the garden of that house" (64).

Pablo Neruda was the universal Chilean, but a much lesser known poet/musician/composer is also evoked. Violeta Parra, neither famous nor politically threatening like the Nobel Prize winning former ambassador and political candidate, is innocuous enough for the Pinochet government to play her work on loudspeakers in public places, listened to by soldiers she would have detested amidst the sound of the curfew warning. Hearing "Gracias a la vida" under those circumstances and recalling her suicide after writing a song celebrating life is more than Littín can bear, suffering as he is, the miracle of that splendid autumn.

The text and the film both depict the violent realities in Chile, but the book also has its moments of humor and also of delicious revenge. Toward the end Littín is becoming increasingly aware of police surveillance and knows he doesn't have much time left. Feeling he is being watched, he follows an old habit of disappearing into a theater in order to think and decide on a course of action. But instead of a film, he has wandered into a tacky night club act, and the stripper singles him out to flirt with as part of her audience participation routine, asking him provocative questions while the spotlight highlights his features to everyone in the room. Cursing his luck, he finally begs her not to ask any more questions as terror makes it impossible for him to uphold his Uruguayan accent and businessman posture. Getting a haircut proves dangerous too, as the hairdresser notices his plucked eyebrows: "Are you prejudiced against gays?" is his defensive retort (51). The barber, following his professional instincts, ignores Littín's precise instructions and follows the natural pattern of his hair growth, leaving him looking too much like Miguel Littín once again. The revenge of the entire two months of filming is highlighted in the episode of filming inside Pinochet's private office and seeing the general pass by within a few feet. A description of the Mapocho River becomes at once a powerful image and political commentary, while reinforcing the French folk wisdom: "Plus ça change, plus c'est la même chose." During and after the bloody coup of 1973 the river was filled with the bodies of victims of the repression. Now, after the totally controlled application of the Chicago school of economics, it is invaded by poor people fighting with dogs for bits of garbage thrown out from the marketplace. So much for the miraculous formulas of Chicago applied to the Chilean economy.

Littín has friends who have stayed behind, and some of them in high places. Just a few days, or even hours, before an interview with a general within the regime who wants to talk, the circle closes in so tightly that the filmmaker knows he has to leave. Willing to turn back even from the airport, the meeting is delayed once again and he cannot risk remaining any longer. He and his companion are dramatically the last to get on the plane, and as

153

they take off, the flight attendant offers them a drink and the information that the police thought an unauthorized passenger had gotten aboard. His reply: "From two who did, *salud*!" (114).

NOTES

1. One of the few critics to include journalism in a study of García Márquez's work is Raymond Williams; see chapter seven of *Gabriel García Márquez* (Boston: Twayne, 1984) 134–54. The French scholar Gilard Jacques has done a number of compilations and studies of the journalism. See *Textos costeños* in the primary bibliography.

2. *Chronicle of a Death Foretold* (New York: Knopf, 1983) 6; all quotations are from this edition and page numbers are noted parenthetically.

4. *Clandestine in Chile* (New York: Holt, 1987) x. All quotations are from this edition.

5. These expressions have lost their García Márquez flavor in the English translation. I have restored "prehistoric" instead of "antediluvian" (56) and "ascended" instead of "went to heaven" (65) for this reason.

CONCLUSION

Gabriel García Márquez's Nobel Prize acceptance speech epitomizes his role as free-lance ambassador for Latin America to the world. It is a plea for peace, for use of the world's wealth to feed the hungry instead of manufacturing more weapons, and specifically for a better understanding of Latin America among Europeans. He sums up, in just a few pages, what the first and second worlds need to know to come to grips in a positive way with the third; he tries to explain, in outline form, the different scales for measuring just about everything in his reality. To do so, he draws on the astonishment of the first Europeans to see the New World, and on the excesses of every sort in contrast with the moderation of Old World: distances, heights, spaces, and incredible chasms between the rich and the poor. He uses statistics sparingly and effectively, often in contrasting Western Europe and Latin America, for he believes that reasonable Europeans, with centuries of history under their belts, are a source of hope for his beloved and beleaguered part of the world. In the effort to explain the aloneness of his fellows he paraphrases his own best-known work: "This is, friends, the knot of our solitude. . . . This is, friends, the size of our solitude." He ends the moving speech on a hopeful note, reopening the spiraled ending of *One Hundred Years of Solitude,* looking toward "a compelling utopia of life, where no one can decide for others even the way they will die, where love will be true and happiness possible, and where races condemned to one hundred years of solitude will finally and forever have a second opportunity on earth."[1]

NOTE

1. "La soledad de América Latina" (Antioquia: Asociación de Profesores, Universidad de Antioquia, 1982–83) pages 3 and 4 of four unnumbered pages. The translations are mine.

SELECTED BIBLIOGRAPHY

So much has been written about García Márquez that selecting works for inclusion in a partial list of secondary sources is always difficult. Since this book is aimed primarily at an American audience, I have included only works in English and only books, special issues of journals devoted to García Márquez and substantial chapters or sections of more general books. There are many fine studies of his work in numerous books and articles in journals both in the U.S. and abroad, but because of limitations of space I have not included them, nor have I included the many dissertations on his work, for they are not as easily available to the nonspecialist. For an extremely detailed comprehensive bibliography on all the work by and about García Márquez, I refer the reader to the two volumes of bibliography by Margaret Eustella Fau (the first volume) and Fau and Nelly Sfeir de Gonzalez (the second) described below.

Works by Gabriel García Márquez

Fiction, Spanish Editions

El amor en los tiempos del cólera (*Love in the Time of Cholera*). Bogotá: La Oveja Negra, 1985.
Cien años de soledad (*One Hundred Years of Solitude*). Buenos Aires: Sudamericana, 1967.
El coronel no tiene quien le escriba (No One Writes to the Colonel). Medellín: Aguirre, 1961.

Crónica de una muerte anunciada (*Chronicle of a Death Foretold*). Bogotá: La Oveja Negra, 1981.

Cuatro cuentos (Four Stories). Mexico: Comunidad Latinoamericana de Escritores, 1974. Contains "Monólogo de Isabel viendo llover en Macondo," "En este pueblo no hay ladrones," "Los funerales de la Mamá Grande," "Un hombre muy viejo con unas alas enormes."

Los funerales de la Mamá Grande (Big Mama's Funeral). Xalapa, Mexico: Universidad Veracruzana, 1962. Contains "La siesta del martes," "Un día de estos," "En este pueblo no hay ladrones," "La prodigiosa tarde de Baltazar," "La viuda de Montiel," "Un día despues del sábado," "Rosas artificiales," "Los funerales de la Mamá Grande."

La hojarasca (Leaf Storm). Bogotá: S.L.B., 1955.

La increíble y triste historia de la cándida Eréndira y de su abuela desalmada (The Incredible and Sad Tale of Innocent Eréndira and Her Heartless Grandmother). Barcelona: Barral, 1972. Contains: "Un senor muy viejo con unas alas enormes," "El mar del tiempo perdido," "El ahogado más hermoso del mundo," "Muerte constante más allá del amor," "El último viaje del buque fantasma," "Blacamán el bueno vendedor de milagros," "La increíble y triste historia de la candida Eréndira y de su abuela desalmada."

Isabel viendo llover en Macondo (Isabel Watching It Rain in Macondo). Buenos Aires: Estuario, 1967. This story is also known as *Monólogo de Isabel viendo llover en Macondo*.

La mala hora (*In Evil Hour*). Madrid: Talleres de Gráficas "Luís Pérez," 1962 (this edition was not authorized by García Márquez). 1st authorized ed. Mexico: Era, 1966.

Ojos de perro azul; nueve cuentos desconocidos (Eyes of a Blue Dog: Nine Unknown Stories). Rosario, Argentina: Equiseditorial, 1971. Contains "La tercera resignación," "La otra costilla de la muerte," "Eva está dentro de su gato," "Amargura para tres sonámbulos," "Diálogo del espejo," "Ojos de perro azul," "La mujer que llegaba a las seis,"

"Nabo, el negro que hizo esperar a los ángeles," "Alguien desordena estas rosas," "La noche de los alcaravanes."

El otoño del patriarca (*The Autumn of the Patriarch*). Barcelona: Plaza & Janes, 1975.

El rastro de tu sangre en la nieve; El verano feliz de la señora Forbes. (A Trace of Your Blood in the Snow; The Happy Summer of Mrs. Forbes.) Bogotá: W. Dampier, 1982. This text has also appeared as *El verano feliz de la Señora Forbes* (Madrid: Almarabu, 1982).

Relato de un naufrago que estuvo diez días a la deriva en una balsa sin comer ni beber, que fue proclamado héroe de la patria, besado por las reinas de la belleza y hecho rico por la publicidad, y luego aborrecido por el gobierno y olvidado para siempre (*The Story of a Shipwrecked Sailor*). Barcelona: Tusquets, 1970. (Report written in 1955).

Todos los cuentos de Gabriel García Márquez (1947–1972). (Complete Stories (1947–1972)). Barcelona: Plaza & Janes, 1975. Contains *Ojos de perro azul, Los funerales de la Mamá Grande,* and *La increíble y triste historia de la cándida Eréndira y de su abuela desalmada.*

Journalistic Works and Interviews in Spanish.

El asalto (The Assault). Managua: Nueva Nicaragua, 1983. El asalto: El operativo con que el FSNL se lanzó al mundo: Un relato cinematográfico. Originally published with the title *Viva Sandino* and subsequently as *El secuestro.*

Así es Caracas (This Is Caracas). Caracas: Ateneo de Caracas, 1980.

La aventura de Miquel Littín clandestino en Chile (The Adventure of Miquel Littín Clandestine in Chile). Madrid: El País, 1986.

Chile, el golpe y los gringos (Chile, the Coup and the Yankees). Bogotá: Latina, 1974.

Crónicas y reportajes (Chronicles and Reports). Bogotá: Instituto Colombiano de cultura, 1976.

Cuando era feliz e indocumentado (When I Was Happy and Undocumented). Caracas: El Ojo del Camello, 1973; Barcelona: Plaza & Janés, 1974.

Cuba en Angola (Cuba in Angola). Tegucigalpa, Honduras: R. Amaya Amador, 1977.

Entre cachacos (Among the Highlanders). Barcelona: Bruguera, 1982; Bogotá: La Oveja Negra, 1983. (Obra periodística).

De Europa y América (From Europe to America). (1955–1960). Barcelona: Bruguera, 1983. (Obra periodística).

García Márquez habla de García Márquez (García Márquez speaks of García Márquez). Bogotá: Rentería, 1979. A collection of interviews and articles published from 1967 to 1979 in various periodicals.

La novela en América Latina: diálogo (The Novel in Latin America: A Dialogue). With Mario Vargas Llosa. Lima: C. Milla Batres, 1968 (?). The dialogue was held on September 4, 1967.

El olor de la guayaba. Conversación con Plinio Apuleyo Mendoza (The Fragrance of the Guava. Conversation with Plinio Apuleyo Mendoza). Barcelona: Bruguera, 1982; Bogotá: La Oveja Negra, 1982.

Operación Carlota (Operation Carlota). Lima: Mosca Azul, 1977.

Periodismo militante (Militant Journalism). Bogotá: Son de Maquina Editores, 1978.

Persecución y muerte de minorías. Dos perspectivas polémicas (The Persecution and Death of Minorities, Two Polemical Perspectives). With Guillermo Nolano-Juárez. Buenos Aires: Juárez, 1984.

Los Sandinistas (The Sandinistas). Bogotá: La Oveja Negra, 1979. Documents and reports by Gabriel García Márquez and others.

El secuestro Relato cinematográfico (The Kidnapping. A Story on Film). Salamanca: Loguez, 1983; Managua, Nueva Nicaragua, 1983. First published as *Viva Sandino* and later as *El asalto.*

La soledad de América Latina ("The Solitude of Latin America"). Speech given in Stockholm 8 Dec. 1982 accepting the Nobel Prize. Antioquia: Asociación de Profesores de la Universidad de Antioqua, 1982–83.

Textos costeños (Coastal Texts). Recopilación y prólogo de Jacques Gilard. Barcelona: Bruguera, 1981; Bogotá: La Oveja Negra, 1983.

De viaje por los países socialistas: 90 días en la "Cortina de hierro" (Traveling in the Socialist Countries: 90 Days Behind the Iron Curtain). Cali, Colombia: Macondo, 1978; Bogotá: La Oveja Negra, 1981. Previously published in the magazines *Cromos,* Colombia, and *Momento,* Venezuela.

Viva Sandino (Long Live Sandino). Managua: Nueva Nicaragua, 1982. Later published as *El secuestro* and *El asalto.*

English Editions

The Autumn of the Patriarch. Trans. Gregory Rabassa. New York: Harper, 1975; paperback rpt. New York: Avon, 1976.

Chronicle of a Death Foretold. Trans. Gregory Rabassa. New York: Knopf, 1983; paperback rpt. New York: Ballantine, 1984.

Clandestine in Chile: The Adventures of Miguel Littín. Trans. Asa Zatz. New York: Henry Holt and Co., 1987.

Collected Stories. New York: Harper, 1984. Originally published separately in three volumes under the titles *Leaf Storm and Other Stories* (1972), *No One Writes to the Colonel and Other Stories* (1968), and *Innocent Eréndira and Other Stories* (1978).

The Fragrance of the Guava: Plinio Apuleyo Mendoza in Con-

versation with Gabriel García Márquez. London: Verso, 1983.

In Evil Hour. Trans. Gregory Rabassa. New York: Harper, 1979. paperback rpt. New York: Avon, 1980.

Innocent Eréndira and Other Stories. Trans. Gregory Rabassa. New York: Harper, 1978; paperback rpt. Harper Colophon, 1979. Contains "The Sea of Lost Time," "The Incredible and Sad Tale of Innocent Eréndira and Her Heartless Grandmother," "Death Constant Beyond Love," "The Third Resignation," "The Other Side of Death," "Eva Is Inside Her Cat," "Dialogue with the Mirror," "Bitterness for Three Sleepwalkers," "Eyes of a Blue Dog," "The Woman Who Came at Six O'clock."

Leaf Storm and Other Stories. Trans. Gregory Rabassa. New York: Harper, 1972; paperback rpt. New York: Avon, 1972. Contains *Leaf Storm,* "The Handsomest Drowned Man in the World," "A Very Old Man with Enormous Wings," "Blacamán the Good, Vendor of Miracles," "The Last Voyage of the Ghost Ship," "Monologue of Isabel Watching It Rain in Macondo," "Nabo."

Love in the Time of Cholera. Trans. Edith Grossman. New York: Knopf, 1988.

One Hundred Years of Solitude. Trans. Gregory Rabassa. New York: Harper, 1970; paperback rpt. New York: Avon, 1970.

No One Writes to the Colonel and Other Stories. Trans. J. S. Bernstein. New York: Harper, 1968; paperback rpt. New York: Avon, 1968. Contains *No One Writes to the Colonel* and *Big Mama's Funeral*: "Tuesday Siesta," "One of These Days," "There Are No Thieves in This Town," "Balthazar's Marvelous Afternoon," "Montiel's Widow," "One Day after Saturday," "Artificial Roses," and "Big Mama's Funeral."

"The Solitude of Latin America: A Nobel Prize Winner Reflects on his Homeland." *Chicago Tribune* (6 Mar. 1983): II, 4.

The Story of a Shipwrecked Sailor. Trans. Randolph Hogan.

New York: Knopf, 1986. Paperback: New York: Vintage Books, 1987.

Critical Works

Books and issues of journals devoted to García Márquez

Alèthea 13 (Spring–Summer 1984). *Gabriel García Márquez: The Man and the Magic of His Writings.* Ed. Ricardo Pastor. This bilingual collection of specialized critical studies represents the proceedings of a symposium held at Saginaw Valley State College in 1983.

Books Abroad 47 (Summer 1973). *Gabriel García Márquez: 1972 Laureate.* Diverse critical articles.

Donoso, José. *The Boom in Spanish American Literature.* Trans. Gregory Kolovakos. New York: Columbia University Press, 1977. A history of the so-called boom in Latin American literature during the 1960s, stating that *One Hundred Years of Solitude* represents the climax of the movement.

Fau, Margaret Eustella. *Gabriel García Márquez: An Annotated Bibliography, 1947–1979.* Westport, CT: Greenwood Press, 1980. The first comprehensive bibliography of the author's works. The compiler includes in the primary sources narrative works, nonfiction articles, and books, movie guides, stories in anthologies, and translations. The secondary sources include bibliographies, books, doctoral dissertations, chapters and sections in books, critical articles, works about the author, and reviews of his books, and an index.

Fau, Margaret Eustella, and Nelly Sfeir de Gonzalez. *Bibliographic Guide to Gabriel García Márquez, 1979–1985.* Westport, CT: Greenwood Press, 1986. This continuation and update of the previous publication completes the detailed compilation of works by and about the author. New categories are audiovisual materials and "Miscellanea," in which the compilers list works, usually brief, which do not fit into their other chapter titles. Together, the set is extremely useful.

Halka, Chester S. *Melquíades, Alchemy and Narrative Theory: The Quest for Gold in "Cien años de soledad."* Lathrap Village, MI: International Book Publishers, 1981. Traces the development of the theme on various levels and uses the interpretation to explain some obscure symbolism.

Interpretaciones a la obra de García Márquez. Ed. Ana María Hernández de López. Monografías de ALDEEU. Madrid: Beramar, 1986. Though the title and some of the essays are in Spanish, most are in English. These critical articles represent the proceedings of a symposium on García Márquez held at Mississippi State University in 1984, focusing on various specialized topics.

INTI: Revista de literatura hispánica 16–17 (Autumn 1982–Spring 1983). *Gabriel García Márquez: Lecturas textuales y contextuales.* Ed. Roger B. Carmosino and Luis B. Eyzaguirre. Includes several specialized critical articles in English.

Janes, Regina. *Gabriel García Márquez: Revolution in Wonderland.* Columbia: University of Missouri Press, 1981. Biography, summaries, and critical comments on fictional work.

Latin American Literary Review 13 (Jan.–June 1985). *Special Issue: Gabriel García Márquez.* Ed. Yvette E. Miller and Charles Rossman. Includes a number of critical articles on specialized themes and four "Meditations, Reflections" by writers John Updike, Alastair Reid, Robert Coles, and Zulfikar Ghose, and a request by García Márquez himself for "lost tales."

McMurray, George R. *Gabriel García Márquez.* New York: Ungar, 1977. The first book-length study of García Márquez in English. The author comments on all his fictional writings and provides plot summaries as well as a bibliography and index.

————. *Critical Essays on Gabriel García Márquez*. Boston: Hall, 1987. A collection of book reviews, essays, and articles from the 1960s to the present. There is a wide representation of critics as well as of works discussed.

Minta Stephen. *Gabriel García Márquez: Writer of Colombia*. London: Jonathan Cape, 1987. Beginning with a very informative and useful chapter on Colombia, the book develops an overview of García Márquez' work within a political as well as literary context. Selected bibliography is arranged according to the book's chapters.

Oberhelman, Harley D. *The Presence of Faulkner in the Writings of García Márquez*. Lubbock: Texas Tech Press, 1980. A short comparison of the two novelists, with bibliography on the subject.

Review: Latin American Literature and Arts. Supplement on Gabriel García Márquez's "One Hundred Years of Solitude." Ed. Ronald Christ. New York: Center for Inter-American Relations, 1976. 101–91.

Schweitzer, S. Alan. *The Three Levels of Reality in García Márquez's "Cien años de soledad."* New York: Plaza Mayor, 1972. The first, immediate level is linear time, the second psychological, and the third mythical, and therefore nonhistorical. The levels constantly interact in the novel.

Sims, Robert Lewis. *The Evolution of Myth in Gabriel García Márquez: From "La hojarasca" to "Cien años de soledad."* Miami: Universal, 1981. Sims applies Claude Levi-Strauss's anthropological models for mythology to the two novels in his study of the evolution of narrative from one to the other.

Shaw, Bradley A., and Nora Vera-Godwin, eds. *Critical Perspectives on Gabriel García Márquez*. Lincoln, NE: Society of Spanish and Spanish-American Studies, 1986. A collection of essays on various works by several scholars.

Williams, Raymond. *Gabriel García Márquez*. Boston: Twayne, 1984. Brief biography and description of works, including commentary on journalism.

Chapters and Sections in Books

Aaron, M. Audrey. "García Márquez' *mecedor* as Link Between Passage of Time and Presence of Mind." *The Analysis of Literary Texts: Current Trends in Methodology.* Ed. Randolph D. Pope. Third and Fourth York College Colloquia. Ypsilanti, MI: Bilingual Press, 1980. 21–30. The rocking chair as symbol in *One Hundred Years of Solitude.*

Acker, Bertie. "Religion in Colombia as Seen in the Works of García Márquez." *Religion in Latin American Life and Literature.* Ed. Lyce C. Brown and William F. Cooper. Waco, TX: Baylor University Press, 1980. 339–50. Colombian Catholicism as seen by García Márquez.

Brotherston, Gordon. "An End to Secular Solitude." *The Emergence of the Latin American Novel.* Cambridge: Cambridge University Press, 1977. 122–35. Focuses on *One Hundred Years of Solitude.*

———. "García Márquez and the Secrets of Saturno Santos." *Contemporary Latin American Fiction: Carpentier, Sabato, Onetti, Roa, Donoso, Fuentes, García Márquez.* Ed. Salvador Bacarisse. Edinburgh: Scottish Academic Press, 1980. 48–53. "Indian engagement" in *The Autumn of the Patriarch* and *One Hundred Years of Solitude.*

Brushwood, John S. *The Spanish American Novel: A Twentieth Century Survey.* Austin: University of Texas Press, 1975. 266–330. Chapters 17, 18, and 19 deal with García Márquez's novels, particularly *One Hundred Years of Solitude,* though the book as a whole traces the development of the novel rather than individual authors.

Foster, David William. "'The Double Inscription of the 'Narrataire' in *Los Funerales de la Mamá Grande*" and "García Márquez and the 'Ecriture' of Complicity: 'La prodigiosa tarde de Baltazar.'" *Studies in the Contemporary Spanish–American Short Story.* Columbia: University of Missouri

Press, 1979. 39–62. Studies of the role of the reader within the text.

Foster, David William, and Virginia Ramos Foster. *Modern Latin American Literature.* 2 vols. New York: Ungar, 1975. 1. 374–91. A collection of periodical reviews of García Márquez's works.

Gallagher, David P. "Gabriel García Márquez." *Modern Latin American Literature.* London: Oxford University Press, 1973. 144–63. Considers all previous work to be preliminaries to *One Hundred Years of Solitude.*

Gerlach, John. "The Logic of Wings: García Márquez, Todorov, and the Endless Resources of Fantasy." *Bridges to Fantasy.* Ed. George E. Slusser, Eric S. Rabkin, and Robert Scholes. Carbondale: Southern Illinois University Press, 1982. 121–29. Study of "A Very Old Man with Enormous Wings."

Harss, Luis, and Barbara Dohmann. "Gabriel García Márquez, or the Lost Chord." *Into the Mainstream.* New York: Harper, 1967. 310–41. This article flows between interview, biography, and criticism. Though there are references to the great work about to come out, it necessarily deals mostly with the early stories and novellas.

Kappeler, Susanne, "Voices of Patriarchy: Gabriel García Márquez's *One Hundred Years of Solitude.*" *Teaching the Text.* Ed. Susanne Kappeler and Norman Bryson. London: Routledge, 1983. 148–63. *One Hundred Years of Solitude* as epic.

MacAdam, Alfred J. "Gabriel García Márquez: A Commodius Vicus of Recirculation." *Modern Latin American Narratives: The Dream of Reason.* Chicago: University of Chicago Press, 1977. 78–87. The reshaping of myths and realities to show the author's personal vision.

———. "Gabriel García Márquez' *Cien años de soledad.*" *Modern American Narration.* Chicago: University of Chicago Press, 1977. 79–83.

Morrison, R. W. "Literature in an Age of Specialization." *Brave New Universe: Testing the Values of Science in Soci-*

ety. Ed. Tom Henighan. Ottawa: The Tecumseh Press, 1980. 112–24. Literature as the depiction of the human experience in a complex society.

Nazareth, Peter. "Time in the Third World: A Fictional Exploration." *Awakened Conscience: Studies in Commonwealth Literature.* Ed. C. D. Narasimhaiah. New Delhi: Sterling, 1978. 195–205. Examples from *One Hundred Years of Solitude* and *The Autumn of the Patriarch.*

Oberhelman, Harley D. "Faulknerian Techniques in Gabriel García Márquez's Portrait of a Dictator." *Ibero-American Letters in a Comparative Perspective.* Ed. Wolodymyr T. Zyla and Wendell M. Aycock. Lubbock: Texas Tech Press, 1978. 171–81. Focuses on *The Autumn of the Patriarch.*

Ondaatje, Michael. "García Márquez and the Bus to Aracataca." *Figures in a Ground: Canadian Essays on Modern Literature.* Ed. Diane Bessai and David Jackel. Saskatoon: Western Producer Prairie Books, 1978. 19–31. Characters and episodes in *One Hundred Years of Solitude.*

Ortega, Julio. *"The Autumn of the Patriarch*: Text and Culture" and *"One Hundred Years of Solitude." Poetics of Change: The New Spanish-American Narrative. Austin: University of Texas Press, 1984. 85–119.* The first is an analysis of *The Autumn of the Patriarch* in its historical and cultural context; the second a look at the elements that form the central structure of *One Hundred Years of Solitude.*

Palencia-Roth, Michael. " 'La primera salida': Gabrial García Márquez: the Alpha and Omega of Myth." *Myth and the Modern Novel.* New York: Garland, 1987. 11–106. The introduction to this work as well as the chapter on García Márquez deal with mythification/demythification in *One Hundred Years of Solitude.*

Rodman, Selden. "Gabriel García Márquez." *Tongues of Fallen Angels.* New York: New Directions, 1972. 113–33. Chronicle of the Rodmans' trip to Aracataca, meeting with the family of García Márquez, and finally with the writer himself.

Rodríguez-Monegal, Emir. "García Márquez: The Long Road to the Nobel Prize." *Contemporary Latin American Culture: Unity and Diversity.* Ed. C. Gail Guntermann. Tempe: Arizona State University, 1984. 95–110. The relationship to folklore and politics.

Rogachevsky, Jorge R. "Individualism and Imperialism in *Cien años de soledad* and *El otoño del patriarca.*" *Politics and the Novel in Latin America: García Márquez and Asturias.* Amherst, NY: State University of New York at Buffalo, 1980. 1–24. The relationships of politics and literature in the two novels.

Schwartz, Kessel. "Sexism in the Spanish American Novel, 1965–1975." *Studies on Twentieth-Century Spanish and Spanish American Literature.* Lanham, MD: University Press of America, 1983. 341–52. Treatments of sex and women in García Márquez's novels.

Siemens, William L. "The Antichrist Figure in Three Latin American Novels." *The Power of Myth in Literature and Film.* Ed. Victor Carrabino. Tallahassee: University Presses of Florida, 1980. 113–21.

Sims, Robert L. "Claude Simon and Gabriel García Márquez: The Conflicts Between *histoire-Histoire* and *historia-Historia.*" *Papers on Romance Literary Relations.* Ed. Cyrus Decoster. Evanston, IL: Northwestern University, 1975. 1–22. Explores the concept of history, official and otherwise, in the two writers.

Tobin, Patricia Drechsel. " 'Everything is Known': Gabriel García Márquez, *One Hundred Years of Solitude.*" *Time and the Novel.* Princeton: Princeton University Press, 1978. 164–91. Reality and imagination in the novel.

Vázquez Amaral, José. "Gabriel García Márquez: *One Hundred Years of Solitude.*" *The Contemporary Latin American Narrative.* New York: Las Americas, 1970. 135–56. Creation of reality by triggering the imagination.

INDEX

170